The Librarian's BOOK of LISTS

Edited by GEORGE M. EBERHART

AMERICAN LIBRARY ASSOCIATION
CHICAGO   2010

CALGARY PUBLIC LIBRARY

P9-DXL-454

George M. Eberhart is editor of the *American Libraries Direct* e-newsletter for the American Library Association. He has been with *American Libraries* magazine since 1996. From 1980 to 1990 he was editor of *College and Research Libraries News,* the news magazine of ALA's Association of College and Research Libraries. Eberhart holds an MLS from the University of Chicago and a bachelor's degree in journalism from The Ohio State University.

ALA Editions purchases fund advocacy, awareness, and accreditation programs for library professionals worldwide.

While extensive effort has gone into ensuring the reliability of information appearing in this book, the publisher makes no warranty, express or implied, on the accuracy or reliability of the information, and does not assume and hereby disclaims any liability to any person for any loss or damage caused by errors or omissions in this publication.

The paper used in this publication meets the minimum requirements of American National Standard for Information Sciences—Permanence of Paper for Printed Library Materials, ANSI Z39.48-1992. ⊗

Library of Congress Cataloging-in-Publication Data
   The librarian's book of lists / edited by George M. Eberhart.
     p. cm.
   Includes bibliographical references.
   ISBN 978-0-8389-1063-4 (alk. paper)
   1. Library science—Miscellanea. 2. Librarians—Miscellanea. 3. Libraries—Miscellanea. 4. Library science—Humor. I. Eberhart, George M.
Z665.L565 2010
020—dc22

                            2009053561

Copyright © 2010 by the American Library Association. All rights reserved except those which may be granted by Sections 107 and 108 of the Copyright Revision Act of 1976.

ISBN-13: 978-0-8389-1063-4

Printed in the United States of America
14 13 12 11 10   5 4 3 2 1

Cover design by Kirstin Krutsch
Text design by Casey Bayer

CONTENTS

INTRODUCTION   vii

5 Things That Make a Library   1

8 Past Predictions about Libraries
and Information in the Future   2

3 Rules of the Librarians of Time and Space   4

10 Suggestions for a Library-Related Ben and Jerry's Flavor   5

10 Gifts for Your Librarian Friends   7

10 Things Microsoft's "Ms. Dewey" Used to Say   9

The Seattle Books Examiner's Top **20** Things
Librarians in Public Libraries Wish Patrons Knew or Did   11

The Swiss Army Librarian's Top **10** Pet Peeves about Patrons   13

10 Commandments for Borrowers of Books   16

6 Birds That Make Library-Related Sounds   18

Larry Nix's Top **10** Libraries on Postage Stamps   19

15 Favorite Library Postcards   21

CONTENTS

Top 10 Library Blogs 27

Top 16 Book Blogs 29

Top 60 Subject Blogs and News Sources 31

Norman Stevens's 10 Best Children's
Picture Books That Feature Libraries and Librarians 40

10 Librarians in Adult Fiction 42

25 Offbeat Book Titles 44

Martha Spear's Top 10 Reasons to Be a Librarian 46

Scott Douglas's 10 Reasons to Be (and Not to Be) a Librarian 47

Top 10 Ways to Make Sure Potential
Applicants for Your Library Job Are Turned Off by Your Ad 49

10 Recruitment Vows for Librarians 51

Roy Tennant's Top 10 Things Library
Administrators Should Know about Technology 52

Leigh Anne Vrabel's 10 Things to Do
When You Are a Library Director 55

Jenny Levine's Mind-Set List for Library School Students 58

Sean Fitzpatrick's 7 Cool Tools That
Librarians Should Know About 60

Key Dates in American Library History 62

5 Movies with the Worst Librarian Stereotypes 67

5 Movies with Librarian Role Models 69

3 TV Shows with Librarians 71

12 Librarians Who Came Back to Haunt 73

Top 15 Books about Real Librarians 76

12 Librarians Who Were Poets 80

14 Ways Public Libraries Are Good for the Country   82

Ranganathan's 5 Laws of Library Science (Updated)   84

Michael Gorman's Revised Laws of Library Science   85

John Cotton Dana's 12 Rules for Reading   86

Top 25 Largest Libraries in North America   88

10 Unusual Rare-Book Genres   90

10 Book Curses   92

10 Intriguing Paper Defects   95

Stephen Leary's Top 10 Ways to Exit a Library   96

Booklist Editors' Best American Fiction, 1980–2005   97

Top 10 Challenged Books, 1990–2000   100

Other Challenged Books, 2001–2009   102

Top 12 Silly Reasons to Ban a Book   104

10 Most Popular Celebrity READ® Posters   106

What to Do When the Media Calls   107

How to Say "Where Is the Library?" in 50 Languages   111

Top 10 Library Music Videos   112

NOTES   115

INTRODUCTION

RECENTLY, MY WIFE and I decided that we would each make a list of ten things we can't live without. It was a fun exercise. Books and libraries were included on mine, along with maps and the Internet, but in the process I realized that "making lists" also belongs in my top ten.

I can remember making list-like notes about books I was reading when I was eleven years old, and when I was thirteen I created a huge time line of anomalous events (UFO sightings, Fortean phenomena, etc.) that I sweet-talked my eighth-grade teacher into mimeographing for some friends. My first book, *The Geo-Bibliography of Anomalies* (Greenwood, 1980), was basically a vast, annotated list, and some of the most popular items in the weekly newsletter I edit, *American Libraries Direct,* are lists like "Ten great graphic novels for young adults" and "One hundred of the best free apps."

A few of the lists that are included in *The Librarian's Book of Lists* have also been featured in *AL Direct.* Most were created especially for the book. All of them, I hope, will be at least tangentially useful and informative, especially for librarians and book lovers. There are lists about the philosophy of librarianship ("14 Ways Public Libraries Are Good for the Country"), the realities of the profession ("10 Pet Peeves about Patrons"), a time line ("Key Dates in American Library History"), libraries on postcards and postage stamps, librarians in the movies and on TV, book curses, censorship ("Top 12 Silly Reasons to Ban a Book"), helpful Internet sites ("Top 60 Subject Blogs and News Sources"), and even some ornithological frippery ("6 Birds That Make Library-Related Sounds"). In short, something for every library listophile.

My deepest thanks go to those who contributed their lists: Danielle Dreger-Babbitt, Brian Herzog, Larry Nix, Norman Stevens, Martha Spear, Scott Douglas, Jennifer Friedman, Roy Tennant, Leigh Anne Vrabel, Sean Fitzpatrick, Jenny Levine, and Stephen Leary. And big thank-yous to editor Chris Rhodes at ALA Editions, who came up with the concept, and to my wife, Jennifer Henderson, who has an amazing ear for errors.

Why can't somebody give us a list of things that everybody thinks and nobody says, and another list of things that everybody says and nobody thinks?

—Oliver Wendell Holmes, "The Professor at the Breakfast-Table," *Atlantic Monthly* (June 1859)

5 THINGS THAT MAKE A LIBRARY

A LIBRARY IS a collection of resources in a variety of formats that is

 ORGANIZED by information professionals or other experts who

 provide convenient physical, digital, bibliographic, or intellectual **ACCESS** and

 offer targeted **SERVICES AND PROGRAMS**

 with the **MISSION** of educating, informing, or entertaining a variety of audiences

 and the **GOAL** of stimulating individual learning and advancing society as a whole.

8 PAST PREDICTIONS ABOUT LIBRARIES AND INFORMATION IN THE FUTURE

01 In 1895, French bibliophile Octave Uzanne predicted that people will be able to "get drunk on literature as if it were fresh water" at kiosks placed at major urban intersections. These "automatic libraries" would vend (for a penny token) a lightweight cylinder (essentially an audiobook) of Dickens, Dumas, or Longfellow that anyone could take home for easy listening.

02 In 1910, a set of 24 trade cards was published in France, credited to an illustrator named Villemard and apparently intended to accompany a food product, showing how life would be in the year 2000. One card, titled "At School," shows a teacher feeding books into a machine, hand-cranked by an assistant, that seems to convert the information in them into a signal transmitted by wires to headphones and skullcaps worn by a roomful of students.

03 In 1922, filmmaker D. W. Griffith, responding to the *New York World* newspaper's question, "A Hundred Years from Now—What?" said: "The great publishing industry will be the publishing of motion pictures instead of print. Motion picture libraries will be as common as private libraries—more so. Theatres will have the same relation to these libraries as the spoken theatre today has to the printed copies of dramatic works. . . . Talking pictures will have been perfected and perhaps have been forgotten again. For the world will have become picture trained so that words are not as important as they are now."

In 1942, Argentine writer Jorge Luis Borges in the short story "The Library of Babel" envisioned the universe as a library composed of unlimited hexagonal galleries, each with four walls of books that contain all possible combinations of letters, spaces, and punctuation marks. Librarians are frustrated because there is no catalog, and no one knows where, or if, any books with coherent text are located.

05 In 1945, Vannevar Bush, director of the U.S. Office of Scientific Research and Development, wrote: "Consider a future device for individual use, which is a sort of mechanized private file and library. It needs a name, and, to coin one at random, 'memex' will do. A memex is a device in which an individual stores all his books, records, and communications, and which is mechanized so that it may be consulted with exceeding speed and flexibility. . . . Wholly new forms of encyclopedias will appear, ready made with a mesh of associative trails running through them, ready to be dropped into the memex and there amplified."

06 In 1965, American computer scientist J. C. R. Licklider wrote: "We need to substitute for the book a device that will make it easy to transmit information without transporting material, and that will not only present information to people but also process it for them, following procedures they specify, apply, monitor, and, if necessary, revise and reapply. To provide those services, a meld of library and computer is evidently required."

 In 1988, library leaders attending the OCLC Conference on the Future of the Public Library listed as one of their greatest hopes that "libraries will finally become identified by the public as the 'information hub' of society because they are gateways to electronic data as well as storehouses of printed materials."

 In 1993, Maurice B. Line, former director-general at the British Library, wrote: "The concept of all information as a public good will have all but disappeared by AD 2015. The private information sector will be very big by AD 2015, and will be carrying out some of the work traditionally carried out by libraries. They will use libraries as sources and pay them commercial rates for this use. They will also work in partnership with libraries in the provision of some services."

3 RULES OF THE LIBRARIANS OF TIME AND SPACE

IN TERRY PRATCHETT'S eighth Discworld novel, *Guards! Guards!*, these rules govern the actions of the librarians in L-space (library space), a dimension connecting all libraries. A large quantity of magical and mundane books create portals into L-space that can be manipulated using special powers taught by the Librarians of Time and Space to those senior librarians deemed most worthy.

01 Silence.

02 Books must be returned no later than the last date shown.

03 Do not interfere with the nature of causality.

AUTHOR		
TITLE		
DATE DUE	**BORROWER'S NAME**	R NU
MR 15 '67		
JA 23 '68		
FE 19 '68		
FE 17 '69		
FE 10 '70		
AP 25 '75		
DEMCO 239		

10 SUGGESTIONS FOR A LIBRARY-RELATED BEN AND JERRY'S FLAVOR

ANDY WOODWORTH, LIBRARIAN at the Bordentown branch of the Burlington County (N.J.) Library System, started a Facebook group in June 2009 to gather support and suggestions to pass on to ice cream makers Ben and Jerry for a library flavor. Here are some favorites.

 01 BOOK BY ITS COVER.** It looks like plain vanilla, but it's actually vanilla with white chocolate swirls mixed in.

 02 CENSOR CHIP.** Vanilla ice cream with red raspberry swirls and chocolate chips.

 03 FREE AND OPEN TO ALL.** A rainbow of flavors with all kinds of chips—butterscotch, peanut butter, chocolate.

 04 GOOEY DECIMAL SYSTEM, 641.862.** Dark fudge alphabet letters with caramel swirls in hazelnut ice cream.

 05 LIBERRY I SCREAM.** Strawberry/blueberry sherbet and vanilla ice cream.

 06 OVERDUE FINE-AS-FUDGE CHUNK.** Hunks of rich fudge brownies in creamy milk chocolate, drizzled throughout with golden caramel and sprinkled with mini white-chocolate coins.

07 RAISIN AWARENESS. Coffee ice cream with raisins and fudge mixed in.

08 REFERENCE RIPPLE. Vanilla with peanut butter inclusions.

09 SH-SH-SH-SHERBET! Key lime sherbet.

10 SINFORMATION DELIGHT. Dulce de leche ice cream swirled with caramel, peaches, and toffee bits.

10 GIFTS FOR YOUR LIBRARIAN FRIENDS

 DIRTY, FLIRTY LIBRARIAN CLOTHES AND ACCESSORIES suggested by fashion expert Lauren Messiah (www.thisnext.com/list/B4EFC8A8/Dirty-Flirty-Librarian). These include a red, navy, and black felt pencil dress by Marc Jacobs; black Scojo rimmed glasses; Positive Red 857 Dior lipstick; a Sonia Rykiel black cardigan; black L'Wren Scott Lady pleat pumps; and a set of Paper Mate number 2 soft lead pencils.

02 GIANT UPHOLSTERED BOOK FURNITURE from Big Cozy Books (www.bigcozybooks.com), designed for durability, safety, and fun by Erik Olofson, who has created benches, booths, tables, seats, wall art, and floor panels in the shape of giant books. They are especially appropriate for children's recreation areas.

03 GUILD OF RADICAL MILITANT LIBRARIANS TOTE BAGS AND T-SHIRTS are available through Instant Attitudes (www.instant attitudes.com/shirts/t052.html). The phrase originated in 2005 when the Electronic Privacy Information Center obtained FBI documents in which FBI agents complained about "radical, militant librarians" while criticizing the reluctance of FBI management to use secret warrants authorized under Section 215 of the USA PATRIOT Act.

 HUMOROUS BOOK COVERS from FlapArt (www.flapart.ca) can amuse or shock staff members and colleagues. Measuring 22 inches by 9¼ inches, the covers will fit most regular-sized hardbacks. Choose from 34 fun titles, including *How to Cheat Your Way through College, How to Murder a Complete Stranger and Get Away with It,* and *Yes I Think You're an Idiot: That's Why I'm Ignoring You.*

05 "LIBRARIAN: THE ORIGINAL SEARCH ENGINE" T-SHIRTS, BUTTONS, MAGNETS, MUGS, STICKERS, NOTE CARDS, AND CAPS (www.cafepress.com/brownbagdesigns/1911390), in Google-like colored letters, from Brown Bag Designs.

06 LIBRARIAN ACTION FIGURE from the Archie McPhee store (www .mcphee.com/shop/products/Librarian-Action-Figure.html) in Seattle. Modeled on former Seattle Public Library Director of Programming Nancy Pearl, the figure features push-button shushing action. A deluxe model comes in a library diorama with a reference desk, computer, book cart, multiple book stacks, and some loose books.

07 A LIBRARY HOTEL WEEKEND in New York City (www.libraryhotel .com). In this small, luxury, boutique hotel located at 299 Madison Avenue and 41st Street, each floor is dedicated to one of the 10 major categories of the Dewey Decimal Classification system. Each of the 60 exquisitely appointed rooms is stocked with books and artwork within a distinct subtopic of the floor's Dewey class.

08 NOVELTY BOOKENDS from Just Bookends (www.justbookends.com) come in all types and shapes. Choose among decorative, children's, or professional styles that include bookends that look like library books, four-bottle wine racks, armillary sundials, classic pedestals, globes, or sports figures.

09 OLD-LEATHER BOOK NECKLACES (www.etsy.com/view_listing .php?listing_id=42558374) are made of specially manufactured, miniature, hand-sewn, leather-bound books. The mini-books, created by Margaux Kent of TheBlackSpotBooks in Philadelphia, as well as her larger creations are made of a "mix of antique and scrap leathers," and the paper is lineless Strathmore artist paper—thick, hand-torn, acid-free pages that work perfectly with ink, pens, pencil, charcoal, and other media.

10 RENAISSANCE LIBRARY CALENDARS (www.renaissancelibrary .com) have been produced since 2001 by Information Strategy and Information Management, a consulting and publishing firm based in Sollentuna, a suburb of Stockholm, Sweden. Each month features a photo of a historic library, selected from nominations submitted by librarians and information professionals in nearly 40 countries.

10 THINGS MICROSOFT'S "MS. DEWEY" USED TO SAY

IN OCTOBER 2006, Microsoft introduced a novelty search engine called Ms. Dewey, which featured a seemingly interactive, vocal, sexy woman with an attitude who stood behind a black desk in front of a cityscape. Presumably a virtual librarian (hence the name), Ms. Dewey would make verbal comments after you entered a search term or if you took too long to type something. She would occasionally use props—sipping a glass of wine while waiting for your input, or doing a mock strip tease if you typed *nudity*. The website was actually a Flash-based, artificial-intelligence interface for Windows Live Search (now Bing), and Ms. Dewey was a series of 600 short videos featuring American actress and musician Janina Gavankar. The search engine was withdrawn in January 2009. Although it was clever and humorous in small doses, the site suffered from poor usability, speed, and search results. Here are some things Ms. Dewey said to searchers.

 "Are you just letting your dog type now?"

 [After a search for "Bill Gates"] "Isn't it funny how preoccupied we get with the lives of others? But you knew that. You're talking to a chick in a computer."

 "You know, when I first saw you, I had a feeling you were going to type in something like that."

 "Of all the searches in the universe, that was definitely . . . one of 'em."

 "Keep asking questions. The more you ask, the more I will know. And soon I will rule the world."

 "You know, it's searches like that that just scream 'Beat me up and take my lunch money.'"

"You are kidding, right? Hey Ricardo, come get a look at what this guy just did a search for."

 "That's interesting in an anthropological kind of way. Would you care to rephrase the question?"

 "Are you as confused as I am? . . . Actually, I'm never confused, but you seem downright flummoxed."

 [Takes a Polaroid photo] "There, I have my photo, and my restraining order is complete."

THE SEATTLE BOOKS EXAMINER'S TOP 20 THINGS LIBRARIANS IN PUBLIC LIBRARIES WISH PATRONS KNEW OR DID

IN 2008, DANIELLE Dreger-Babbitt, writer and adult/teen librarian at the Mill Creek branch of the Sno-Isle Regional Library System in Snohomish County, Washington, took an informal poll of librarians she knew in Boston, Dallas, Detroit, Indianapolis, New York City, and Portland, Oregon, about what they wished library patrons knew or did. This list appeared in her Seattle Books Examiner column for the Examiner.com news site.

 01 ENOUGH WITH THE "SEXY LIBRARIAN" JOKES. We've heard them all before.

 02 ASK US FOR WHAT YOU REALLY WANT. Be specific.

 03 ASK US WHAT WE READ. We are supposed to give recommendations.

 04 DO NOT LEAVE YOUR CHILD (OR CHILDREN) UNATTENDED. Stranger Danger exists everywhere.

 05 COME TO OUR PROGRAMS. They are free entertainment for the whole family.

 06 PLEASE RESPECT THE DESK BARRIER. Wait for us to turn the computer screen around so that you can see what information we've found for you.

 07 WE LIKE IT WHEN YOU THANK US. It reminds us that all of our hard work is worth it.

 08 PLEASE BE PATIENT WITH US. Chances are you won't have to wait very long before it's your turn.

TURN OFF YOUR CELL PHONE WHEN YOU COME TO THE DESK. It's rude, plain and simple.

 THE LIBRARY HAS ALMOST AS MANY DVDS AS YOUR LOCAL VIDEO STORE. Why subscribe to Netflix when you can rent from the library?

 LET US KNOW WHAT MATERIALS YOU'D LIKE TO SEE ON THE SHELF. We really try to buy what you like to read, watch, and listen to.

 PRACTICE GOOD HYGIENE. Please try to sneeze away from the computer or reference desk.

PLEASE LISTEN TO US THE FIRST OR EVEN SECOND TIME WE SAY SOMETHING. This goes for when we answer a reference question or ask you to lower your voice.

IF POSSIBLE, CHECK OUT ALL MATERIALS AT ONCE. It helps avoid a backup at the circulation desk or self-checkout station.

 TELL US WHAT YOU LIKE AT THE LIBRARY. It's the only way we can make changes.

 RETURN YOUR ITEMS ON TIME. Keeping library materials past their loan period ties them up.

 PAY YOUR FINES. Almost everyone (even librarians) has had late items at one time or another.

 BE RESPECTFUL OF OTHER LIBRARY PATRONS. This includes giving the person ahead of you at the reference desk enough space, not yelling at your kids across the room, talking on your cell phone at the computer, and swearing.

 WE SUPPORT INTELLECTUAL FREEDOM. We believe that it is the parent's or guardian's responsibility to monitor what [her] children take out of the library.

USE US. Don't let an economic crisis keep you and your family from having fun. Do your holiday shopping at a library book sale; attend library programs, lectures, and author talks; check out new DVDs, CDs, video games, and best sellers; and use the free Wi-Fi. The library will continue to offer these things as long as you use them.

THE SWISS ARMY LIBRARIAN'S
TOP 10 PET PEEVES ABOUT PATRONS

BRIAN HERZOG, HEAD of reference at Chelmsford (Mass.) Public Library, compiled this list of bad patron behavior for his *Swiss Army Librarian* blog in 2009. He writes: "Usually I'm a pretty happy-go-lucky guy, and I really do enjoy my job. But I thought I'd share a list of the top 10 things that patrons do that can really irk me. Not that I expect every patron interaction to be perfect and wonderful, of course; these are just a few things that make bad days worse."

01 PATRONS WHO DON'T WAIT IN LINE. When I'm helping someone at the reference desk, common sense tells me that if another person walks up, they'd stand behind the person I'm helping to wait their turn. However, in practice, instead of lines, people tend to form huddles. They will stand almost next to the person I'm helping, eliminating all privacy for the first patron. The longer people have to wait, the more they inch closer to the desk—to the point where they tap their keys on the desk or volunteer answers to the first patron's question. I always try to make eye contact with people and tell them I'll be right with them, but they often take that as an invitation to ask their question—even if I'm on the phone.

02 PATRONS WHO DON'T END PHONE CALLS WITH "GOODBYE." I suppose this isn't necessarily limited to libraries, but I've never experienced it anywhere but while at work. I'll answer a patron's question, there will be a little awkward silence, and then I'll start saying something like, "is there anything else I can do," and halfway through I just hear *click*.

03 PATRONS WHO WON'T STOP ASKING THEIR QUESTIONS LONG ENOUGH FOR ME TO ANSWER. Maybe this one is due to patrons thinking their question is very complex, when in reality it's not. After the first sentence or two I'll have an answer or resource for them, but they keep elaborating and I can't get a word in edgewise. I don't like interrupting people, but sometimes there is no other option.

04 PATRONS WHO STAND IN FRONT OF THE PRINTER. This only bothers me when someone comes to the desk and says the printer is broken. Fair enough, it happens. So they ask if I can fix it, and lead me over to the printer. But then they proceed to walk right up to the printer and stand in front of it, blocking me from getting to it. More often than not, I actually have to ask the patron to move.

05 PATRONS WITH NO CELL PHONE ETIQUETTE. Cell phones aren't banned from my library—we just ask people to use them politely. Here's one cell phone conversation that I overhear repeatedly: [*Patron is sitting at a computer, when suddenly some horrible digital song starts playing very loudly from their bag. After a minute of struggling, they finally get their cell phone out and answer it:*] "Hello? . . . I can't talk right now, I'm in the library. . . . No, I can't talk. . . . I'm in the library. . . . I don't know, later. . . . No, I can't talk. . . . I can't talk. . . . I don't know, maybe Bob. . . . I'm in the library, I can't talk. . . . I'll call you back. . . . Around 3, and Bob and Mary. . . . How about Taco Bell? . . . Look, I'm in the library, I'll call you back. . . . I can't talk, I'm in the library. . . . The library. . . . I can't talk. . . . I'll call you back. . . . Okay, bye. . . . Bye. . . . I'll call you back. . . . Okay, bye." So here's my question: If you can't talk because you're in the library, why do you even answer the phone? And of course, they never turn the ringer down, so a few minutes later their bag is blaring again. Sigh.

06 PATRONS WHO TRY TO HIDE THAT THEY'RE USING A CELL PHONE. Again, my library allows cell phone use. But some patrons come in and try to hide that they're on their cell phone by holding their whole hand open over the phone. Maybe we're just supposed to think they enjoy touching their cheek and ear simultaneously, and looking at desk staff out of the corner of their eye. The good thing is that these people are always speaking quietly, but it annoys me that they think they can get away with something by hiding it.

PATRONS WITH BAD CLOSING-TIME ETIQUETTE. I'm sure any public place that closes at a certain hour has people that come in a minute before closing time. We certainly do, and we also have patrons who stay on the computers right up to closing time. But the ones who really bug me are the people who get up off their computers while I'm trying to do all my closing-time tasks, then stand at the desk and talk to me about the other patrons who are still on the computers and how they make it harder for us to close the library because they just refuse to leave. I guess they just miss the irony of the situation.

PATRONS WHO ARE PASSIVE-AGGRESSIVE. We have a good collection, but we certainly don't have a book on everything. For instance, a patron will ask for a book on megalodon, the extinct giant shark. We don't have a book just about that, but after searching through indexes, I can find information about that shark in a more general book on fossils. It's exactly what the patron needs, but their response is, "Well, I guess it'll work, but too bad you don't have a book just about megalodon sharks." I also get the feeling sometimes that people blame me personally for not having written a book on their topic—the history of their house, how supportive families are when a child is born in Peru, etc.

 PATRONS WHO HAVE A BOOK'S CALL NUMBER OR TITLE WRITTEN ON A PIECE OF PAPER, AND ASK IF I CAN HELP THEM FIND IT, BUT THEY HOLD THE PAPER SO THEY CAN READ IT BUT I CAN'T. Eventually patrons graduate from this habit to setting the paper down on the desk. But invariably, they set the paper down facing them—which actually is fine, because I've gotten quite good at reading upside-down. But what I can't do is read in-motion, and this is a drawback because as soon as the patron realizes the paper is facing them, they start spinning it and moving it so that it faces me. While nice and considerate, it'd actually be quicker if they didn't.

PATRONS WHO SAY I SHOULD HAVE BEEN A TEACHER. I usually hear this after I finish showing someone how to do something on a computer. I know they mean this as a compliment, but it sort of implies that being a librarian is unfortunate somehow. I'm a librarian because I want to be a librarian; if I weren't, then I wouldn't have been here to show them all the stuff I just showed them.

10 COMMANDMENTS FOR BORROWERS OF BOOKS

HENRY T. COUTTS was a librarian at the Islington Public Library in England during the early twentieth century. His humorous *Library Jokes and Jottings* included a number of insightful sketches on the library profession, including this tongue-in-cheek Decalogue.

 01 Thou shalt not buy what thou canst borrow.

 02 Thou shalt take care of thine own books, for thy babies and thy puppies will find as much delight in borrowed books as playthings.

 03 Thou shalt not cut the leaves of a book with a butter-knife, nor decorate the margins with jam in imitation of the old illuminated manuscripts.

 04 Remember that the most artistic form of appreciation is to repair the torn leaves of a book with postage stamp edging, and to arrange the red and green lines alternately.

 05 Honor the opinions of an author as expressed in his book, but shouldst thou disagree with his views, pencil thine own notes in the margins. By so doing thou wilt not only give evidence of thy vast learning, but will irritate subsequent readers who will, unmindful of thy superior knowledge, regard thee as a conceited ass.

 06 Thou shalt choose thy books from amongst those most worn. Shouldst thou be dissatisfied with their contents thou wilt have the pleasure of knowing that many of thy neighbors have been "had" likewise.

 07 Thou shalt consult the librarian when thou knowest not what thou requirest. Should he be unable to assist thee, substitute "in" for "con."

Thou shalt not pay fines on principle (current cash is much to be preferred).

 Thou shalt not bear false witness against the library assistant, saying: "He taketh the best books and reserveth them for his friends."

 Thou shalt not covet the books that thy neighbor hath appropriated.

6 BIRDS THAT MAKE LIBRARY-RELATED SOUNDS

01 BEWICK'S WREN (*Thryomanes bewickii*), a native of North America, is the deaccessionist of this group. It has a harsh, scratchy call of *weed-it weed-it*.

02 The BROWN GERYGONE (*Gerygone mouki*), a warbler-like bird of eastern Australia, has two distinct songs. In the south, it seems to work at the reference desk, with an incessant, busy call of *what-is-it, what-is-it*. In the north, it more likely has a job in the teen center, sounding off with *having-a-good-time*.

03 The RED-WATTLED LAPWING (*Vanellus indicus*), found in India and Southeast Asia, could be a mystery novel readers' advisor. Its call is a loud, distinctive *did-he-do-it*.

04 The SOUTHERN BOOBOOK (*Ninox novaeseelandiae*) is a hawk-owl of New Zealand and Australia. It makes one of the best-known nocturnal bird sounds in Australasia: a loud *book-book*.

05 The WESTERN WHIPBIRD (*Psophodes nigrogularis*) is a crested, olive-green bird of southern Australia. It must have a school library background, because the male calls out a scratchy *it's-for-teacher*, to which the female responds *pick-it-up*.

06 The YELLOW-HEADED WARBLER (*Teretistris fernandinae*), found only in Cuba, makes a noisy, rasping *shhh-shhh-shhh-shhh-shhh-shhh*. You knew there would be one somewhere.

LARRY NIX'S TOP 10 LIBRARIES ON POSTAGE STAMPS

RETIRED LIBRARIAN, LIBRARY History Buff blogger, and ardent philatelist Larry Nix has been collecting postage stamps depicting libraries and librarians (a hobby called bibliophilately) since 1995. Here's what he says about the 10 shown here: "Postage stamps are a reflection of history, contemporary culture, and the value that society places on the subject of the stamp. Regrettably, out of the hundreds of thousands of postage stamps that have been issued since Great Britain's Penny Black in 1840, there have only been a few hundred featuring libraries. I have chosen a representative group that has a special appeal to me because of the library's significance, the unusual nature of the library or service depicted, and the design of the stamp. Because of their contributions to society, libraries (and librarians) deserve to be featured on more postage stamps in the future."

01 BELGIUM, Scott #B43 (1918), Library of the Catholic University of Louvain. This library was destroyed in both World Wars I and II. This stamp serves as a tribute to the resilience of all libraries that have suffered significant damage because of fire, water, or war.

02 BRITISH VIRGIN ISLANDS, Scott #784 (1993), bookmobile. Issued as part of the golden jubilee of secondary education and library services, this stamp is one of only seven that depict that romantic vehicle of library outreach, the bookmobile.

03 CANADA, Scott #173 (1930–1931), Library of Parliament in Ottawa. Built in 1876, this library is a Canadian icon that appears on several postage stamps and the Canadian $10 bill.

04 DENMARK, Scott #1162 (1999), Extension of the Royal Library. Completed in 1999, this dramatic building known as "The Black Diamond" has an outside cover of black marble and glass.

05 EGYPT, Scott #1790 (2001), Bibliotheca Alexandrina. The dream of reviving the fabled ancient Library of Alexandria became a reality in 2002 when the building on this stamp was completed with support from Egypt, other Arab states, and UNESCO.

06 FAROE ISLANDS, Scott #39 (1978), original building of the National Library of the Faroe Islands. One of more than 1,000 stamps designed for several different countries by world-renowned master engraver Czesław Słania (1921–2005).

07 ICELAND, Scott #400 (1968), National Library of Iceland, Reykjavik. I like this stamp commemorating the 150th anniversary of Iceland's National Library because it shows people using the library.

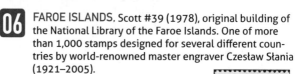

08 MAURITIUS, Scott #1011 (2005), Carnegie Library at Curepipe, the second-largest town on the island. Of the 2,509 library buildings Andrew Carnegie helped build in the English-speaking world, this library is only one of five to appear on a government-issued postage stamp.

09 UNITED NATIONS, OFFICES IN NEW YORK, Scott #592 (1991), Dag Hammarskjöld Library at UN headquarters. This library (the building in the foreground) appears on more postage stamps than any other library in the world. The stamp was also designed by Czesław Słania.

10 UNITED STATES, Scott #2004 (1982), Thomas Jefferson Building, Library of Congress. Promoted by Librarian of Congress Daniel Boorstin and designed by noted graphic artist Bradbury Thompson, this stamp was the first in the United States to commemorate a library for its role as a library.

15 FAVORITE LIBRARY POSTCARDS

POSTCARDS ARE AN invaluable visual resource for cultural historians and a still-affordable hobby for those who like to collect things. A close look at a postcard can reveal a wealth of information—small, barely noticeable details on the image side; nuances of meaning in the message; trivia in the printed caption; postal history in the cancellation and the postage; and significance in the credits for the artist, photographer, publisher, and printer. It can be absorbing fun to try to sleuth out the date based on signage, automobiles depicted, the context of a message, or other subtle clues when a card's year of publication is missing. Libraries on postcards are a logical collecting avocation for librarians who value the rich history of their profession.

Although I do not rigorously collect library postcards, I have run across many unusual examples in antique stores and postcard shows that I just couldn't resist acquiring. These are my favorites.

01 **DAWSON CITY (YUKON) CARNEGIE LIBRARY.** This classic public library was built with the help of a $25,000 grant from philanthropist Andrew Carnegie. The image on the card shows 28 prominent citizens standing on its steps on opening day, August 16, 1904, the building trimmed with British Union flags, a U.S. flag draped in one window, and "Carnegie Library" set in gleaming gold letters above the entrance. At the time, the library was considered the most elaborate building in Dawson and housed more than 5,000 books. Unfortunately, the Klondike Gold Rush had ended five years earlier and the population had dwindled from 40,000 to 5,000. The library moved out after a fire in 1920, but the building, the northernmost Carnegie Library anywhere, still stands as a Masonic lodge.

02 **WIDENER LIBRARY, HARVARD UNIVERSITY, CAMBRIDGE, MASSACHUSETTS.** The centerpiece of the Harvard library system, the Widener opened June 24, 1915, and commemorates Harry Elkins Widener, a Harvard graduate, book collector, and victim of the *Titanic* disaster in

1912. This card shows what the General Reading Room looked like at 10:45 one morning in its first year. Hats, suits, and ties were universal student garb at the time. When the library was rededicated after a five-year, $92 million makeover in 2004, this reading room regained much of its initial splendor.

03 BRITISH MUSEUM READING ROOM, LONDON. The great circular reading room of the British Library, designed by Sydney Smirke based on a sketch by Chief Librarian Anthony Panizzi, was in continuous use by such notables as V. I. Lenin, Karl Marx, Rudyard Kipling, George

Bernard Shaw, Bram Stoker, Edward Elgar, and William Butler Yeats from 1857 to October 25, 1997, when the library moved to the new facility in St. Pancras. Its original color scheme of light blue, cream, and gold leaf was restored in 2000 when the room reopened as the Paul Hamlyn Library within a huge, canopied Queen Elizabeth II Great Court.

04 EISENHOWER PRESIDENTIAL LIBRARY AND MUSEUM, ABILENE, KANSAS. Most presidential library postcards show the exterior or the museum part of the facility, but this one shows Ike and Mamie standing in the book-filled Presidential Room during their visit of November 30, 1967, one year after the library opened for research. The library stands near the site of Eisenhower's boyhood residence in Abilene.

President and Mrs. Dwight D. Eisenhower

05 ILLINOIS STATE LIBRARY, SPRINGFIELD. Illinois Governor George H. Ryan, in office from 1999 to 2003 (and since 2007 serving time in federal prison for racketeering and fraud), expanded state funding for education and school infrastructure to record levels. In 1999, he created a Governor's Office on Literacy, which promoted a "Read Together, Grow Together" campaign spearheaded by Secretary of State Jesse White and the Illinois State Library. This ISL postcard shows a family of robots reading together.

06 AMERICAN LIBRARY ASSOCIATION CAMP LIBRARY, CAMP SHELBY, HATTIESBURG, MISSISSIPPI.

Shortly after the United States entered World War I in 1917, ALA was invited to provide library facilities for army and navy training camps. Camp Shelby soldiers are reading books and magazines in the ALA library, a "favorite corner" of the camp. A sign encourages them to "Take one to your tent, Read it and pass it on." The camp was deactivated at the end of the war, shortly after this card was mailed on December 9, 1918, but it was in use again in World War II and the Korean War, and in 1956 it was designated a permanent training site.

07 SOLDIER'S HOME LIBRARY, SANDUSKY, OHIO.

Completed in 1888, this state veterans' facility accommodated 1,400 men in its heyday and consisted of 34 buildings made of "blue limestone and practically fire-proof." In 1910, when this postcard was mailed, the facility offered housing and care for Civil War and Spanish-American War veterans from Ohio. Now known as the Ohio Veterans Home, most of the old buildings have been replaced with modern facilities that are home to some 660 residents. The library building had deteriorated significantly and was torn down in the early 1990s. The Veterans Hall of Fame stands on the site now.

08 CREDITON PARISH CHURCH LIBRARY, DEVON, ENGLAND.

The chained books shown on this card from the 1910s constitute a rare example of a church library featured on a postcard. Crediton Parish Church has a long history (in fact, it celebrated its 1,100th anniversary in 2009). The library was founded by the Rev. Thomas Ley, vicar from 1689 to 1721, who donated books from his own collection. The majority of them date from the seventeenth century, although there are two incunabula from the fifteenth. The chained books shown here are in a rather sad state of deterioration. It's likely that the damage occurred in the nineteenth century when the church had the volumes on display for curious antiquarians. The practice of chaining books for protection in British academic libraries had begun to die out by the mid-seventeenth century and even earlier in church libraries. The Crediton church collection was transferred on permanent loan to the University of Exeter Library in 1968. Christine Faunch, acting head of archives and special collections at Exeter, informs me that the volumes shown could be from the great Polyglot Bible of Bishop Brian Walton, printed in 1655–1657, which shows evidence of chaining and collapsed pages.

09 BRITISH COUNCIL LIBRARIES. The British Council, established in 1934, is the U.K. government's cultural arm overseas. It still operates libraries that promote English language and culture in many countries, although many of them have closed in recent years, especially in Europe and Latin America. This British Post Office card shows one of a set of four postage stamps issued September 25, 1984, to commemorate the fiftieth anniversary of the Council.

10 ATLANTIC MUTUAL INSURANCE COMPANY, MARINE LIBRARY, NEW YORK CITY. Established in 1842, Atlantic soon became the largest marine insurance firm in North America. This postcard from the early 1960s shows its famed library, which housed the largest repository of records on marine disasters outside the United Kingdom. The caption notes, "Victorian horsehair sofa and chairs were made for Atlantic a century ago." Housed in the Atlantic Building at 45 Wall Street from 1959 to the early 1970s, the company moved to 140 Broadway after the World Trade Center was built; its offices are now split between 100 Wall Street and Madison, New Jersey. According to the March 13, 1964, issue of *Life* magazine, the library once had a room devoted to memorabilia about the brigantine *Mary Celeste*, a ship it had insured that was found mysteriously abandoned on the high seas in December 1872. The library's marine disaster books

were so legendary, one story goes, that someone once wrote in and asked if it had a record of Noah's Ark. A waggish employee supplied the following record: "Built 2448 B.C. Gopher wood, pitched within and without. Length, 300 cubits; width, 50 cubits; height, 30 cubits. Three decks. Cattle carrier. Owner: Noah and Sons. Last reported stranded Mount Ararat."

11 RUINS OF STANFORD UNIVERSITY LIBRARY, STANFORD, CALIFORNIA.

The San Francisco earthquake of April 18, 1906, also took a toll on Stanford, some 30 miles south of the city. One major casualty was the new university library, which had just been completed in the summer of 1905 but was not yet occupied. As an exhibition noted 100 years later, "Unfortunately, librarians were not consulted during the design process, the floor plan was unsuitable for use, and fire protection for the books was inadequate. Structural problems were also discovered. As the university trustees moved to correct these, the earthquake hit and the effect was utter ruin." The wings of the building were destroyed, but its dome was left undamaged. The university had to demolish the structure and start over; luckily, the collection was intact in its old quarters. The Graduate School of Business now stands on the site.

12 FLOODED DEFIANCE (OHIO) PUBLIC LIBRARY.

Five days of unusually heavy rains throughout Ohio in late March 1913 caused rivers to overflow their banks and levees, resulting in widespread, record flooding. Hundreds of people drowned. The Defiance Public Library, located near the confluence of the Auglaize and Maumee Rivers, was inundated along with 268 other homes as the Maumee crested 10 feet above flood stage. The library, a Carnegie building dedicated in July 1904, survived the flood and is still in use today.

13 JEWISH THEOLOGICAL SEMINARY OF BRESLAU (NOW WROCŁAW, POLAND), LIST OF SEMINARY BOOKS.

This rabbinical seminary, founded in 1854, was the first modern institution for the training of German rabbis. It was destroyed by the Nazis in 1938, but after World War II some of its materials wound up in Polish and Russian museums, archives, and libraries. This postcard is one of a set of 20 published by the All-Russian State Library for Foreign Literature in Moscow in 2003 as part of a joint effort with the Research Project on Art and Archives in the United States to identify, catalog, exhibit, and translate manuscripts from the seminary that are held in Russia. Only 39 items were found, making their recovery all the more valuable.

14 **JAPAN LIBRARY ASSOCIATION, STATEMENT ON INTELLECTUAL FREEDOM IN LIBRARIES.** This could be the only instance where a library association statement has appeared on a postcard. The JLA's intellectual freedom statement, revised in 1979, is different in form but similar in sentiment to both the ALA Library Bill of Rights and its Freedom to Read statement. The statement appears in full on JLA's website in an English translation (www.jla.or.jp/jiyu/english.html).

15 **NATIONAL LIBRARY BOARD OF SINGAPORE, LIBRARY MANNERS CONTEST.** In September 1999, Singapore's National Library Board held a contest to promote good behavior in the island's libraries. All you had to do was call a phone number and answer two questions about politeness in order to qualify to win one of four $50 book vouchers or one of 150 video CDs featuring Singaporean actor and comedian Moses Lim. Under the heading "Good Library Manners for a Better Library," this postcard offers and illustrates some politeness tips: Do not crowd around computer terminals or tables. Take only those books you need. Handle books with care. Speak softly or whisper. Do not use phones and pagers. Walk, do not run. The card was distributed on free postcard racks throughout the city.

TOP 10 LIBRARY BLOGS

IF YOU ONLY have time to read 10 library-related blogs, these are the ones you should add to your RSS feed. Of course, there are many other interesting, informative, thought-provoking, and clever blogs to choose from, and new ones are added every week or so. But these cover the core issues of librarianship.

01 **ACRLOG** (http://acrlblog.org). Steven Bell (Temple University), Barbara Fister (Gustavus Adolphus College), and other regular contributors cover the full spectrum of issues facing academic libraries. Though technically an official blog of the Association of College and Research Libraries (an ALA division), it is pretty light on association business. Topics include technology issues, scholarly communications, professional development, faculty and student issues, ethics, and information literacy.

02 **DAVID LEE KING** (www.davidleeking.com) is digital branch and services manager at the Topeka and Shawnee County (Kans.) Public Library. His eponymous blog ranges from building the library user experience to web design and other social-media strategies.

03 **ILIBRARIAN** (http://oedb.org/blogs/ilibrarian/). Ellyssa Kroski, information services technologist at Barnard College, locates many cool lists, how-to's, resources, and tips on information technology and apps and summarizes them here.

04 **IN THE LIBRARY WITH THE LEAD PIPE** (http://inthelibrarywiththe leadpipe.org). Six librarians who work in academic, public, and school libraries across the United States (as well as their guests) post in-depth essays that explore new ideas in librarianship, document problems, and suggest solutions. Topics encompass information literacy, outreach, special collections, and libraries as a public good.

05 LIBRARIAN.NET (www.librarian.net), written by Jessamyn West, has been "putting the rarin' back in librarian" since April 1999 with news and insights, making it one of the first personal biblioblogs. West writes about creative library services, open source software, usability, access, and copyright, and she pulls no punches when she sees a program or service run ineptly.

06 LIBRARY HISTORY BUFF BLOG (http://libraryhistorybuff.blogspot .com) is a companion blog to the website of retired Wisconsin librarian and postal-history aficionado Larry Nix, who writes about famous librarians of the past, significant libraries and archives throughout history, old library technology, libraries on postage stamps, library ephemera, and library humor.

07 LISNEWS (www.lisnews.org) was created in November 1999 by librarian Blake Carver as a place to post links to library and information science news. He now has a bevy of bloggers who add content when they find something interesting or informative in the mainstream media or blogosphere. The site also hosts LISTen podcasts on library and tech topics and an LIS news wire.

08 PLANET CATALOGING (http://planetcataloging.org). Designed and maintained by Jennifer W. Baxmeyer and Kevin S. Clarke, this site is a one-stop shop for blog posts related to cataloging and metadata. Content is automatically picked up from such sources as Catalogablog, Metadata Matters, The FRBR Blog, 025.431: The Dewey Blog, Thingology, and other essential reads.

09 RESOURCESHELF (www.resourceshelf.com) is updated daily by an editorial team headed by Gary Price and Shirl Kennedy, who summarize and comment on articles, reports, databases, surveys, product announcements, statistics, government documents, and other new online resources that reference librarians and researchers need to know about.

10 STEPHEN'S LIGHTHOUSE (http://stephenslighthouse.com). Stephen Abram, vice president of strategic partnerships and markets for publishing house Gale Cengage, looks at trends in technology and social media, information marketing and economics, and web services and products.

TOP 16 BOOK BLOGS

MANY ONLINE RESOURCES review and comment on new books and literature. Some cover all types of books, others specialize in children's or young adult literature, while others are eclectic. Here are some of the best.

 ABBY (THE) LIBRARIAN (http://abbylibrarian.blogspot.com). Abby Johnson, children's librarian at the New Albany–Floyd County (Ind.) Public Library, provides in-depth book reviews and news about anything related to kid-lit.

 AWFUL LIBRARY BOOKS (http://awfullibrarybooks.wordpress.com) is a hilarious blog dedicated to hopelessly out-of-date or cluelessly inappropriate books found in real public libraries. Mary Kelly, adult services librarian with the Salem–South Lyon (Mich.) District Library, and Holly Hibner, adult services coordinator for the Plymouth (Mich.) District Library, have no end of fun with titles like *What to Do When the Russians Come* (1985) that should have been weeded long ago.

THE BOOK SMUGGLERS (http://thebooksmugglers.com). Thea James and Ana Grilo comment jointly on romance, gothic, fantasy, and sci-fi titles, with summaries of their favorite TV shows mixed in.

BOOKGASM (www.bookgasm.com), subtitled "Reading material to get excited about," covers all kinds of genre fiction, from horror and sci-fi to mystery and suspense, graphic novels, and pulp fiction. Edited by Oklahoma City writer Rod Lott, the site allows you to group reviews by your favorite genre.

BOOKLIST ONLINE (www.booklistonline.com). ALA's premier review magazine offers an excellent online component that even nonsubscribers to the service can take advantage of. Features and literature roundups are here in droves. It also boasts a family of blogs that focus on children's books (*Bookends*), audiobooks (*Audiobooker*), reference materials (*Points of Reference*), book group suggestions (*Book Group Buzz*), and what *Booklist* reviewers do (*Likely Stories*).

BOOKSLUT (www.bookslut.com). Founded in 2002 as a literary blog and webzine by critic and reviewer Jessa Crispin, *Bookslut* now has many contributors for its iconoclastic, witty, and readable adult fiction and nonfiction reviews, features, interviews, and columns.

A FUSE #8 PRODUCTION (www.schoollibraryjournal.com/blog/1790000379.html). New York Public Library children's librarian Elizabeth Bird's sense of humor shines through in her lively reviews of kids' (and some young adult) books. On Sundays she posts videos.

 GALLEYCAT (www.mediabistro.com/galleycat/) is the book-publishing blog of Mediabistro.com, a website for media professionals. Here you'll find news about publishers, book release parties, author gossip, awards shortlists, video reviews, contests, and bookseller news.

 GUYS LIT WIRE (http://guyslitwire.blogspot.com) is a group effort by librarians and writers who review books for teenage boys. It's not all explosions and thrillers; they include many thoughtful titles.

 I'M HERE. I'M QUEER. WHAT THE HELL DO I READ? (www.leewind.org) discusses young adult books with gay, lesbian, bisexual, transgender, questioning, and queer characters. Editor Lee Wind also shares fascinating quotes and poems from GLBTQ history.

 LIBRARIAN BY DAY (http://librarianbyday.blogspot.com). Melissa Rabey, a young adult librarian at the Frederick County (Md.) Public Library, serves up a nice selection of reviews of teen novels.

 THE PLANETESME PLAN (http://planetesme.blogspot.com). Esmé Raji Codell, author of *Educating Esmé: Diary of a Teacher's First Year* (1999), reviews her favorite books for kids, especially ones that are good for reading aloud.

 STACKED (http://stackedblog.com). Booklovers Christina Oppold and Marcelo Teson and young-adult reviewer Veronica Wong edit this blog about the fiction and nonfiction they happen to be reading, both new and old; even *Huck Finn* and *Mein Kampf* turned up one month.

 THE STORY SIREN (www.thestorysiren.com). Dental assistant Kristi focuses on young adult novels in this fun blog that includes author interviews and book giveaways.

A STRIPED ARMCHAIR (http://astripedarmchair.wordpress.com). Voracious reader Eva examines her recent read-a-thon titles.

THINGS MEAN A LOT (www.thingsmeanalot.com). An intriguing book blog by Ana Silva, a soon-to-be library student in Portugal, who reviews fantasy, fairy tales, mythology, young adult and children's books, and comics.

TOP **60** SUBJECT BLOGS AND NEWS SOURCES

LIBRARIANS MUST MAINTAIN their reputations (whether deserved or illusory) for knowing a little bit about every subject imaginable. Although we usually have specialties in one or two topics, there comes a time when we need to apply our knowledge-management skills to an unfamiliar discipline. As a rule, we tend to be better in the areas of literature, education, technology, and the arts, while we are weaker in history, the physical and life sciences, law, and economics. And sports—fuhgeddaboudit. Here are 60 topical blogs and other online resources that will keep you informed in most disciplines; if you manage to make the rounds every one or two weeks, your patrons will revere you as a twenty-first-century polymath (aka Renaissance man or woman).

ARTS

 ALLMUSIC BLOG (http://blog.allmusic.com) has fewer posts than other music blogs, but it features a wide range of genres (even classical) and has the advantage of being only one click away from the companion *AllMusic, AllMovie,* and *AllGame* sites.

 ART OBSERVED (http://artobserved.com) covers news about exhibitions, installations, auctions, and other events in the art world, with an emphasis on New York and London. The sidebar has links to artists (both living and deceased), galleries, museums, collectors, and other art sources.

 ARTSJOURNAL (www.artsjournal.com). Douglas McLennan, a former arts reporter in Seattle, puts together numerous links to news stories and hosts a bundle of associated blogs on art, music, dance, theatre, media, publishing, and ideas.

 BIBLIODYSSEY (http://bibliodyssey.blogspot.com) consists of thematic collections of historic book illustrations put together by Australian bibliophile Paul K. Recent topics have included mushrooms, anatomy, alchemy, fantasy, fashion, flora, book covers, and maps.

A DAILY DOSE OF ARCHITECTURE (http://archidose.blogspot.com). New York City architect John Hill provides photos, commentary, reviews, and links about modern architecture.

DESIGN OBSERVER (www.designobserver.com) offers short essays and articles on graphic design, communications arts, print, typography, and criticism by a group of design writers and numerous contributors.

 HOLLYWOOD ELSEWHERE (http://hollywood-elsewhere.com). Written by film critic Jeffrey Wells, this is one of the best general-interest movie blogs ever, packed with stills, trailers, videos, reviews, Oscar predictions, and insider insights.

 IO9 (http://io9.com) is an innovative site that covers all things science fiction and horror, with a liberal dose of real science and futurism mixed in. Edited by Annalee Newitz, io9 reviews TV episodes, new films, books, comics, art, quotes, and humor. Sci-fi continues to be one of the most innovative literary genres because it explores the human response to future technologies, unexpected events, and alternate realities.

HUMANITIES

BIBLICAL STUDIES AND TECHNOLOGICAL TOOLS (http://bibleand tech.blogspot.com). Gettysburg College Biblical Studies professor Mark Hoffman gathers news about Bible software, online maps of the Holy Land, language resources, and other Internet reference material.

CIVIL WAR MEMORY (http://cwmemory.com). History teacher Kevin Levin blogs broadly about Civil War military and social history, history education and interpretation, slavery, Southern culture, and historians.

THE HISTORY BLOG (www.thehistoryblog.com) is primarily about European history from ancient times through the Renaissance, as well as the provenance, preservation, and disposition of antiquities and other artifacts.

HISTORY NEWS NETWORK (http://hnn.us). A project of the Center for History and New Media at George Mason University in Virginia, this site offers a weekly roundup of news and original articles on issues in American and European history from a wide range of ideological views. Book reviews are also included.

LANGUAGE LOG (http://languagelog.ldc.upenn.edu/nll/) is a thoughtful and humorous blog maintained by University of Pennsylvania linguist Mark Liberman that covers misuse of language and linguistics in the media, syntax, slang and taboo vocabulary, and misstatements by usage pundits.

 MEDIEVAL NEWS (http://medievalnews.blogspot.com) includes articles on medieval history, art, society, architecture, literature, and discoveries.

 SHORPY (www.shorpy.com) consists of an online archive of thousands of high-resolution photos from the 1850s to the 1950s. Its namesake, Shorpy Higginbotham, was a teenager who worked in an Alabama coal mine in the early twentieth century. The site is actually a blog that posts photos on a daily basis and keeps them archived and searchable. Each photo links to a high-resolution image.

 THE SPLINTERED MIND (http://schwitzsplinters.blogspot.com) offers personal reflections on the philosophy of psychology, culture, and experience by Eric Schwitzgebel, professor of philosophy at the University of California, Riverside.

LAW AND POLITICS

 ABOVE THE LAW (www.abovethelaw.com). Containing news and gossip about the legal profession, law schools, and court cases, this blog was established by former federal prosecutor David Lat for the Breaking Media network of sites.

 BESPACIFIC (www.bespacific.com) serves up law and technology news with links to primary and secondary sources on such topics as e-government, privacy, government documents, cybercrime and ID theft, the PATRIOT Act, freedom of information, federal legislation, and legal research. It was launched in 2002 by law-firm librarian and legal technologist Sabrina I. Pacifici.

BLOG OF RIGHTS (www.aclu.org/blog), published by the American Civil Liberties Union, covers news about free speech, privacy, discrimination, racial justice, immigration, illegal detention, and other human rights issues.

20 COMMON DREAMS (www.commondreams.org) brings together news and commentary from a progressive, green viewpoint. Founded by Craig Brown and the late Lina Newhouser in 1997, the site features op-eds from progressive writers and activists and links to other resources.

21 MILITARY BLOGS (http://military-blogs.military.com) aggregates postings from U.S. defense, military policy, weapons, and soldier blogs, including DoD Buzz, Defense Tech, and Military Education Blog.

22 TALKING POINTS MEMO (www.talkingpointsmemo.com) is an up-to-the-minute political blog created and run since 2000 by journalist Josh Marshall. *Time* magazine named it best blog of 2009. Its primary focus is an intelligent analysis of U.S. foreign and domestic policy, and it features high-profile guest bloggers and enthusiastic reader-commenters. A spin-off blog, *TPM Muckraker,* investigates political corruption.

23 THE VOLOKH CONSPIRACY (http://volokh.com). UCLA law professor Eugene Volokh and his academic colleagues offer commentary, primarily libertarian and conservative, on U.S. legal and political issues.

SCIENCE AND TECHNOLOGY

24 ARS TECHNICA (http://arstechnica.com) covers technology trends, Apple and Microsoft news, open source software, popular science, and gaming developments, along with editorial comment and analysis.

25 BAD ASTRONOMY (http://blogs.discovermagazine.com/bad astronomy/). Astronomer and skeptic Phil Plait maintains this blog as an adjunct to his book, *Bad Astronomy: Misconceptions and Misuses Revealed, from Astrology to the Moon Landing "Hoax"* (Wiley, 2002), to clear up misconceptions about astronomy and space science in movies, the news, and print, and on the Internet.

26 CHEMISTRY BLOG (www.chemistry-blog.com). UC-Berkeley chemistry graduate student Mitch André Garcia and friends blog about developments in chemistry.

27 CRYPTOMUNDO (www.cryptomundo.com). Author Loren Coleman provides news and informed discussion on cryptozoology—reports and rumors of animals new to science.

ENERGYWISE (http://spectrum.ieee.org/blog/energy/renewables/energywise/). *IEEE Spectrum News* editor Bill Sweet produces this blog on green power, biofuels, energy, and climate change.

 GEOTRIPPER (http://geotripper.blogspot.com) offers many photographs of geological formations in the Western United States taken on field trips by Garry Hayes, geology teacher at Modesto (Calif.) Junior College, plus speculation on earthquakes, volcanism, and other earth science topics.

 KEVINMD.COM (www.kevinmd.com/blog/) was voted the best medical weblog of 2008. Written by Kevin Pho, a practicing physician in Nashua, New Hampshire, this lively blog covers credible health-care and medical news of practical use to patients.

 NOT EXACTLY ROCKET SCIENCE (http://blogs.discovermagazine.com/notrocketscience/). Ed Yong is a science writer based in London who reports on recent scientific research in clear, understandable language. Topics include animal behavior, environmental science, psychology, neuroscience, evolution, genetics, molecular biology, and medicine.

 PHYSICS ARXIV BLOG (www.technologyreview.com/blog/arxiv/) is a *Technology Review* blog that summarizes the best ideas from the Physics arXiv online forum on which physicists post preliminary research findings.

 READWRITEWEB (www.readwriteweb.com). Launched in 2003 by New Zealander Richard MacManus, *ReadWriteWeb* reports on trends in web technology, new apps, social networking, and mobile computing.

 THE RURAL BLOG (http://irjci.blogspot.com) is a digest of news, trends, and issues about rural America, from the Institute for Rural Journalism and Community Issues based at the University of Kentucky. Topics include economic development, rural broadband, agriculture and farming, biotechnology, and renewable energy.

 SCIENCE DAILY (www.sciencedaily.com) is the best website for news in all fields of the physical, biological, earth, and applied sciences, and it is updated several times a day. Articles and news releases are sortable by subfield (such as nanotechnology, origin of life), and the site groups videos, images, and reference articles on various disciplines.

SPACE WEATHER (www.spaceweather.com). Tony Phillips compiles daily data on observable atmospheric and astronomic events, including auroras, sunspots and solar flares, meteors and fireballs, comets, near-earth asteroids, and planetary conjunctions. Readers also submit photos of unusual solar halos, rainbows, and orbiting spacecraft.

TETRAPOD ZOOLOGY (http://scienceblogs.com/tetrapodzoology/). British editor and vertebrate paleontologist Darren Naish blogs about dinosaurs, other extinct animals, and animal behavior.

TREEHUGGER (www.treehugger.com). Hosted by the Discovery Channel, *TreeHugger* is maintained by an international team of writers and editors who comment on green news, sustainable solutions, and environment-friendly products.

UNDERWATER TIMES (www.underwatertimes.com) is a constantly updated compilation of news and features on marine life, oceanography, scuba diving, and undersea exploration, edited by scuba diver and underwater photographer Jeff Dudas.

SOCIAL SCIENCES

ARCHAEOLOGICAL NEWS (www.archaeology.org/news/). This *Archaeology* magazine site provides headlines and links to news about archaeological excavations, discoveries, and speculation.

BLOG ABOUT STATS (http://blogstats.wordpress.com). Armin Grossenbacher at Statistics Switzerland created this blog in 2006 for statisticians to share their experiences, focus attention on new developments, and review information releases from statistical organizations.

BUSINESS INSIDER (www.businessinsider.com) brings together a wide range of business news and analysis, grouped into sections on technology, the stock market, media, the economy, green tech and energy, business strategy, and business law. The site's editor-in-chief is Henry Blodget, a former securities analyst for Merrill Lynch.

ECONOMICS ROUNDTABLE (www.rtable.net/index/rt/economics/recent/). Economics professor William R. Parke of the University of North Carolina, Chapel Hill, maintains this aggregator of economic news that covers the political spectrum.

ESCHOOL NEWS (www.eschoolnews.com) covers all aspects of K–20 education technology—legislation and litigation, case studies, best practices, library issues, reports and statistics, and new products. The website is a companion to the weekly print newsletter.

 THE ESSENTIAL READ (www.psychologytoday.com/blog/essentials/) selects the best posts from the many topical blogs that accompany the *Psychology Today* magazine website.

 EVERYDAY SOCIOLOGY BLOG (http://nortonbooks.typepad.com/everydaysociology/) offers a sociological take on news events and trends. Developed by University of Southern California sociologist Karen Sternheimer, this blog includes discussion on crime, popular culture, population, social psychology, and statistics.

 FREAKONOMICS (http://freakonomics.blogs.nytimes.com) is a companion blog to the popular *Freakonomics* books by journalist Stephen J. Dubner and University of Chicago economist Steven D. Levitt. Hosted by the *New York Times,* it applies economic theory to such wide-ranging topics as taxation, prostitution, abortion, the environment, crime, and health care.

 THE FRESHXPRESS (http://thefreshxpress.com) provides news and commentary from a young African American perspective on politics, personalities, culture, sex, sports, and finances.

 GENEA-MUSINGS (www.geneamusings.com). Genealogist and retired space engineer Randy Seaver supplies genealogy research tips and techniques, news and commentary, humor, and family-history research and stories in this link-packed blog.

 GOOGLE MAPS MANIA (http://googlemapsmania.blogspot.com) covers new map mash-ups, tools, and applications created by map fans worldwide using Google Maps, Google Earth, UMapper, or other cartographic software. Edited by London web designer Keir Clarke, the blog showcases both useful and offbeat maps, from satellite tracking in street view to a zombie outbreak simulator.

 INSIDE HIGHER ED (www.insidehighered.com) showcases college and university news, feature stories, columns, career advice, and 10 associated blogs.

LIFEHACKER (http://lifehacker.com) features tips, shortcuts, and software downloads that help you get things done smarter and more efficiently, whether it's screencasting, video editing, diagnosing hard drive problems, knowing when to buy an extended warranty, or using a spoon to prevent milk from boiling over.

 MY LATINO NEWS (http://mylatinonews.com) aggregates news and information relevant to the Hispanic community. Popular topics include immigration, entertainment, politics, and discrimination.

 NATIVE UNITY (http://nativeunity.blogspot.com), edited by retired print journalist Bobbie Hart O'Neill, brings together news articles, features, and op-ed pieces on all aspects of Native American life and culture in the United States and Canada.

 NEUROANTHROPOLOGY (http://neuroanthropology.net), a collaborative blog for anthropology and the brain sciences, was created by Greg Downey at Macquarie University. The field of neuroanthropology embraces all dimensions of human neural activity, including emotion, perception, cognition, motor control, and skill acquisition. The blog offers a roundup of current news every Wednesday and other anthro news throughout the week.

 ROMENESKO (www.poynter.org/column.asp?id=45). American journalist Jim Romenesko runs this journalism and media-industry blog hosted by the Poynter Institute. It's a good website to watch in an era when print newspapers and magazines face new challenges and online media creates additional niches.

 SETH GODIN'S BLOG (http://sethgodin.typepad.com). Author, entrepreneur, and marketer Seth Godin offers a wealth of ideas on creative marketing, clear communications, human behavior and cognition, and organizational strategies.

THE ANOMALIST (www.anomalist.com). Publisher and researcher Patrick Huyghe edits this daily review of world news about scientific anomalies and historical mysteries—UFOs, cryptozoology, psychic phenomena, reincarnation cases, pyramid mysteries, out-of-place archaeological artifacts, and other events, conditions, behavior, and discoveries that do not conform to prevailing paradigms.

BOING BOING (http://boingboing.net) is an award-winning popular-culture blog established in 2000 by Mark Frauenfelder, who was later joined by coeditors Cory Doctorow, David Pescovitz, and Xeni Jardin. Frequent topics include tech commentary, gadgets, free speech and privacy issues, science fiction, fringe culture, and cool stuff in general. Google and other Internet tracking sites show it as one of the most linked-to blogs in the world.

 MENTAL FLOSS BLOG (www.mentalfloss.com/blogs/) serves as the online accompaniment to *Mental Floss* magazine, an eclectic mix of facts, trivia, weird news, quizzes, interesting video clips, lists, and humor on many topics.

NORMAN STEVENS'S 10 BEST CHILDREN'S PICTURE BOOKS THAT FEATURE LIBRARIES AND LIBRARIANS

01 CARI BEST, *Red Light, Green Light, Mama and Me* (New York: Orchard, 1995). Niki Daly, illus. As a librarian, Mama sets a good example for her daughter as well as for the readers.

02 EVE BUNTING, *Our Library* (New York: Clarion, 2008). Maggie Smith, illus. Children love anthropomorphic animals—especially when they run the library.

03 BARBARA COONEY, *Miss Rumphius* (New York: Viking, 1982). The classic tale of an environmentally conscious librarian who spreads flowers to make the world beautiful.

04 CARMEN AGRA DEEDY, *The Library Dragon* (Atlanta: Peachtree, 1994). Michael P. White, illus. The school librarian, Miss Lotta Scales, is a monster of a dragon . . . or is she?

05 AMY HEST, *The Babies Are Coming!* (New York: Crown, 1997). Chloë Cheese, illus. Children are never too young to go to the library; even babies are welcome.

06 PAT MORA, *Tomás and the Library Lady* (New York: Knopf, 1997). Raul Cólon, illus. The true story of a young boy whose library experience leads to an academic career.

07 SARAH STEWART, *The Library* (New York: Farrar, Straus, and Giroux, 1995). David Small, illus. Elizabeth's collection of books grows so big she turns her house into a library.

MIKE THALER, *The Librarian from the Black Lagoon* (New York: Scholastic, 1997). Jared D. Lee, illus. See what happens to kids who talk in the library.

 ANN WARREN TURNER, *The Pumpkin Cat* (New York: Hyperion, 2004). Amy June Bates, illus. Libraries and cats naturally go together, and Halloween is just the right setting.

 SUZANNE WILLIAMS, *Library Lil* (New York: Dial, 1997). Steven Kellogg, illus. A formidable librarian becomes a role model who takes on, and conquers, a motorcycle gang.

10 LIBRARIANS IN ADULT FICTION

01 CHARLES A. GOODRUM, *Dewey Decimated* (New York: Crown, 1977). After accusations of a forged Gutenberg Bible surface at Washington, D.C.'s Werner-Bok Library, retired librarian Edward George helps piece together a tale of theft, fraud, and murder. Other Werner-Bok who-dunits are *Carnage of the Realm* (1979) and *A Slip of the Tong* (1992).

02 MICHAEL GRIFFITH, *Bibliophilia: A Novella and Stories* (New York: Arcade, 2003). Middle-aged Louisiana State University librarian Myrtle Rusk is tasked with patrolling the stacks to tell lustful students to take their hormones elsewhere. But she bends the rules for Seti, an Egyptian student worker with an amusing misgrasp of English who has fallen for the wiles of Lili, the library director's sensuous daughter.

03 MINDY KLASKY, *Girl's Guide to Witchcraft* (Don Mills, Ontario: Red Dress Ink, 2006). In lieu of a pay raise, Jane Madison, a librarian at the Peabridge Free Library in Washington, D.C., moves into free lodging— a dusty cottage on the library grounds—where she stumbles upon a long-forgotten collection of books on witchcraft. She soon unleashes a wealth of hidden powers. "They don't teach witchcraft in library school. Vermin—check. Mold and mildew—check. Difficult patrons— check. But there was no course in witchcraft, no syllabus for sorcery. If only I'd been properly prepared for my first real job."

04 ALLEN KURZWEIL, *The Grand Complication* (New York: Theia, 2001). Bibliophile Henry James Jesson III hires New York Public Library reference librarian Alexander Short to identify the missing object in an eighteenth-century cabinet of curiosities. Involved in the intrigue is George Speaight, the curator of the erotica-oriented Center for Material Culture, whose nickname is "The Librarian of Sexual Congress."

05 SEAN MCMULLEN, *Souls in the Great Machine* (New York: Tor, 1999). This is the first novel in the author's Greatwinter Trilogy, set in a postapocalyptic fortieth-century Australia where twenty-first-century technology is only a vague memory. The ambitious librarian Zarvora Cybeline designs a steampunk computer called the Calculor, powered by abacus-wielding human prisoners, intended to save the world from another Ice Age. She works for the Libris, a powerful library system in which—despite violent duels over rival classification systems—librarians attempt to reconstruct long-forgotten electrical machinery. Followed by *The Miocene Arrow* (2000) and *Eyes of the Calculor* (2001).

06 AUDREY NIFFENEGGER, *The Time Traveler's Wife* (San Francisco: MacAdam/Cage, 2003). Henry DeTamble works at Chicago's Newberry Library when he isn't inadvertently flipping into the past or the future (an affliction called Chrono-Displacement Disorder). A footnote: The Newberry does own an uncataloged book allegedly bound in human skin (p. 133), although a recent analysis by the conservation staff has led them to believe the binding is in fact highly burnished goatskin.

07 JASON SHIGA, *Bookhunter* (Portland, Ore.: Sparkplug Comics, 2007). Special Agent Bay and his squad of professional library police (bookhunters) have less than three days to track down a rare 1838 Bible stolen from the Oakland (Calif.) Public Library. Set in 1973 when library technical services were dependent on paper records, this graphic novel is an action-packed spoof of police procedurals. Shiga based the library on both the Oakland main library and the old Berkeley central library.

08 JAMES TURNER, *Rex Libris, Volume 1: I, Librarian* (San Jose, Calif.: SLG Publishing, 2007). Two-fisted title character Rex Libris was a librarian at the ancient Library of Alexandria who became traumatized by its destruction. Ever since, he has fought the forces of evil, destroyed monsters, and protected books and library patrons. He now works for Head Librarian Thoth at the Middleton Public Library, fighting ignorance with the help of coworkers Circe and Hypatia as well as his amazing teleportation crystals. *Volume 2: Book of Monsters* (2009) continues the series taken from the 13 issues of Turner's comic.

09 JINCY WILLETT, *Winner of the National Book Award: A Novel of Fame, Honor, and Really Bad Weather* (New York: Thomas Dunne, 2003). The bookish yet witty Dorcas Mather, librarian at the Squanto Library in Frome, Rhode Island, reads and comments on a biography of her tartish twin sister Abigail, who happens to be in jail for the murder of her husband.

10 LAURALI ROSE WRIGHT, *A Touch of Panic* (New York: Penguin, 1995). Cassandra Mitchell, librarian of Sechelt, British Columbia, helps her Mountie boyfriend, Staff Sergeant Karl Alberg, solve local crimes. In this book, she is stalked by Gordon Murphy, a wealthy but psychopathic library science professor from the University of British Columbia who spotted her at a conference and decided she was the perfect one for him.

25 OFFBEAT BOOK TITLES

 RONALD A. BECK AND FRED BECK, *I Fought the Apemen of Mt. St. Helens* (n.p.: The authors, 1967).

 CHRISTOPHER I. BRANCH, *Fighting a Long Nuclear War* (Washington, D.C.: National Defense University, 1984).

 JIM BULLARD, *Looking Forward to Being Attacked* (Memphis?: The author, 1977).

 EVELYN CHEESMAN, *Six-Legged Snakes in New Guinea* (London: George G. Harrap, 1949).

 KAZ COOKE, *Living with Crazy Buttocks* (Ringwood, Vic.: Penguin Books Australia, 2001).

 THEATA IONA CROWE, *How to Cook a Bigfoot* (Hillsboro, Ore.: Western Bigfoot Society, 2000).

 ADAMS FARR, *The Fangs of Suet Pudding* (London, 1944).

 PETER HANSARD AND BURTON SILVER, *What Bird Did That? A Driver's Guide to Some Common Birds of North America* (Berkeley, Calif.: Ten Speed Press, 1991).

 DAVID HEATLEY, *My Brain Is Hanging Upside Down* (New York: Pantheon, 2008).

 GARY LEON HILL, *People Who Don't Know They're Dead* (Boston: Weiser, 2005).

 GEORGE HOWSON, ed., *Handbook for the Limbless* (London: The Disabled Society, 1921).

 DOMINIQUE LAPORTE, *History of Shit* (Cambridge, Mass.: MIT Press, 2000).

13 TONY LESCE, *Escape from Controlled Custody* (Port Townsend, Wash.: Loompanics, 1990).

 14 P. L. H. MCSWEENEY, *Cheese Problems Solved* (Cambridge, Eng.: Woodhead, 2007).

 15 KATE MARSDEN, *On Sledge and Horseback to Outcast Siberian Lepers* (New York: Cassell, 1892).

 16 JULIAN MONTAGUE, *The Stray Shopping Carts of Eastern North America: A Guide to Field Identification* (New York: Abrams Image, 2006).

 17 CHRISTOPHER MOORE, *Island of the Sequined Love Nun* (New York: William Morrow, 1997).

 18 JAMES W. MOSELEY AND KARL T. PFLOCK, *Shockingly Close to the Truth! Confessions of a Grave-Robbing Ufologist* (Amherst, N.Y.: Prometheus, 2002).

 19 LEWIS OMER, *Hand-Grenade Throwing as a College Sport* (New York: Albert G. Spalding, 1918).

 20 ADAM QUAN, *How to Date a White Woman: A Practical Guide for Asian Men* (Vancouver, B.C.: Technobase, 2002).

 21 JACK SCAGNETTI, *Movie Stars in Bathtubs* (Middle Village, N.Y.: Jonathan David, 1975).

 22 ALISA SURKIS AND MONICA NOLAN, *The Big Book of Lesbian Horse Stories* (New York: Kensington, 2002).

 23 MIKE TECTON, *How I Cured Deadly Toe Nail Fungus* (McLean, Va.: The author, 1997).

 24 SHERRY VELASCO, *Male Delivery: Reproduction, Effeminacy, and Pregnant Men in Early Modern Spain* (Nashville, Tenn.: Vanderbilt University, 2006).

 25 DOUGLAS B. VOGT, *Gravitational Mystery Spots of the United States: Explained Using the Tof Multidimensional Reality* (Bellevue, Wash.: Vector Associates, 1996).

MARTHA SPEAR'S TOP 10 REASONS TO BE A LIBRARIAN

LIBRARY MEDIA SPECIALIST Martha J. Spear came up with these reasons after one of her former students told her she was pursuing a master's degree in museum studies. Spear writes: "Congratulating her, I jokingly said, 'Watch it. That's awfully close to a master's in library science.' She laughed and said: 'Oh, I'd never do that.'" But librarianship does have much to offer, so here are Spear's 10 reasons why the profession is worth pursuing.

 IT'S EVER-CHANGING AND RENEWING. We work with exciting people, we have to do nearly everything, and we learn something new every day.

 THE ROMANCE. We meet exciting colleagues in a stimulating environment.

 LEARN USEFUL SKILLS. We help students write a paper on the Manhattan Project, or we find out the best place to buy a teakettle online.

 GREAT CONFERENCES. What better way to see the world and recharge your professional batteries?

 TIME OFF. We may not get great pay, but we do generally receive liberal vacations.

 A JOB WITH SCOPE. It's not just a desk job, and it's anything but routine.

 IT PAYS THE RENT. It has allowed me to support myself moderately well and be employable in different markets and in changing times.

 GOOD WORKING CONDITIONS. In a library, we are clean, dry, warm, and working with people who are generally happy to be there.

 COOL COWORKERS. We are intelligent, cultured, well-read people who bring a myriad of skills, backgrounds, and interests to the job.

 GRAND PURPOSE. We support the freedom to read and the right to access information for all people.

SCOTT DOUGLAS'S 10 REASONS TO BE (AND NOT TO BE) A LIBRARIAN

IN RESPONSE TO a *U.S. News and World Report* article that declared "librarian" to be one of the best jobs of 2008, Scott Douglas, librarian at Anaheim (Calif.) Public Library, compiled these lists.

TEN REASONS TO BE A LIBRARIAN

 You totally get to classify things.

 Where else are you going to ruin a person's day over a 20-cent fine?

 The funky glasses make you easily mistaken for a hipster.

 You can make up whatever you want and people will believe you just because you're a librarian.

 You get first dibs on unclaimed items in the lost-and-found box.

 You get to be in charge of buying furniture that is least likely to show a piss stain.

 Playing Scrabble on the Internet can be considered "professional development."

 The most stressful thing that happens is arguing with people over why they cannot view their favorite pornography website.

 You get to spend two hours designing a sign that says the library will be closed for the holidays.

 No one says anything when you fall asleep during a meeting.

TEN REASONS NOT TO BE A LIBRARIAN

 Who wants to go to grad school for two years to learn theory you will never use?

 Those little punk teenagers on skateboards.

 People kind of expect you to know things.

 If you know enough about how to find information to be a good librarian, you can definitely make more money doing something else.

 People automatically assume that you have some weird fetish for cats.

 People expect you to help them find things when you are not working just because you know how.

 Some people think you are weird because you classify things in your house—like clothes and dishes.

 Writing library policy can be about as fun as watching paint dry.

Every great idea you have is likely to get shot down as soon as someone says, "Let's form a committee to decide things."

At some point in your career, someone will, or will try to, physically assault you over something incredibly lame (like not giving him or her more time on the Internet).

TOP **10** WAYS TO MAKE SURE POTENTIAL APPLICANTS FOR YOUR LIBRARY JOB ARE TURNED OFF BY YOUR AD

JENNIFER FRIEDMAN, PATIENTS' librarian at the Mendota Mental Health Institute in Madison, Wisconsin, wrote this important checklist in 1996 when she was working in Bismarck, North Dakota. Of course, job ads are now more often online than in print, but these blunders are still made.

01 BEGIN YOUR AD with a spunky, funky ode to the community in which you live, praising its [beaches, low sales tax, educated residents, well-known colleges, mild climate, arts community, growing economy, etc.], especially when your community is widely thought to be an undesirable place to live anyway.

02 REQUIRE A SUBJECT MASTER'S for a nonspecialist position when your college is absolutely unknown and accepts any kid that applies. Same goes for a tech school or junior college.

03 REQUIRE A SUBJECT MASTER'S for a nonspecialist position when the salary you offer is below $30,000/year. A subject master's *costs* more than that.

04 REQUIRE REFERENCE LETTERS to be sent along with the application if your deadline is short. You will end up weeding out the best applicants merely because their reference people take longer to write better-thought-out letters.

05 ASK FOR A CURRICULUM VITAE when you know perfectly well all you will get is a résumé with the words "Curriculum Vitae" across the top.

06 OFFER LITTLE OR NO INFORMATION ABOUT THE JOB. "Librarian for midsized college" is a heading, not a job description. Give us food for our imaginations, at least!

07 GIVE A DEADLINE that's five days after the publication date of the publication the ad is in, figuring that the very best people will hurry and get their applications in online or overnight. No, the most *desperate* people will hurry and get their applications in online or overnight.

08 MISSPELL KEY WORDS in the ad: aquisitions, cereals librarian, colections, supervizion, refernece.

09 PUT TOGETHER AN UTTERLY UNREALISTIC AD. just to see if you can find any poor saps who can fit your requirements: "Branch head, inner city area, must have MLS, subject master's in linguistics, advanced coursework in diplomacy, ability to dodge bullets, skill in glass repair. Salary: $20,500/year."

10 LEAVE OUT A CONCRETE SALARY NUMBER by saying only "commensurate with experience." Or just don't bother mentioning a salary, because you know people are so desperate for jobs that they won't care how little you'll pay them. You can think up an appropriately insulting number after the interview, or make something up after hearing whether they sound stupid over the phone. This is preying upon the job force and betrays the fact that everyone in your administration thinks librarians are menial workers. It hurts all of us.

10 RECRUITMENT VOWS FOR LIBRARIANS

THE PROFESSION OF library and information science always needs fresh minds willing to tackle complex new problems. In 2004, Emma Bradford Perry, dean of libraries at Southern University in Baton Rouge, Louisiana, drew up this list of recruitment vows for professionals.

Take responsibility for the future of our profession:

 MAKE A PERSONAL COMMITMENT TO RECRUITMENT AND DIVERSITY, and encourage your colleagues to do the same.

 DEVELOP A POSITIVE VISION AND THINK CREATIVELY in ways that will excite potential students.

 REACH OUT, ENCOURAGE, COACH, AND COUNSEL potential students.

 PROVIDE ONGOING PROFESSIONAL AND EMOTIONAL SUPPORT AND ASSISTANCE to library school students.

 DEVELOP ONE-ON-ONE RELATIONSHIPS with non-degreed library staffers and others, encouraging them to consider librarianship as a career.

 PROVIDE AS MUCH FLEXIBILITY AS POSSIBLE to accommodate subordinates pursuing an MLS.

 ENCOURAGE AND PARTICIPATE IN THE DEVELOPMENT AND IMPLEMENTATION OF A FIRST-RATE MENTORING PROGRAM in your institution.

 GET TO KNOW and work closely with a library school dean and staff.

 BRANCH OUT FROM TRADITIONAL SETTINGS to capture the attention of potential library school students.

RECRUIT ACTIVELY, not passively.

ROY TENNANT'S TOP 10 THINGS LIBRARY ADMINISTRATORS SHOULD KNOW ABOUT TECHNOLOGY

ROY TENNANT, SENIOR program manager for OCLC Programs and Research at Mountain View, California, compiled this list in 2009 for his *TechEssence .info* blog. He writes: "It's not insulting to say that those who run libraries tend not to know all that much about technology. A very different set of skills is needed to run an organization, and those skills do not often come packaged along with technical knowledge and experience. But administrators need to know some specific things about technology in order to do their jobs well. Effective use of technology in libraries is too important to not get right."

01 TECHNOLOGY ISN'T AS HARD AS YOU THINK IT IS, at least compared to years ago. Any reasonably competent library technologist can take a server from scratch to a fully functioning website in a day. And with services like Amazon's Elastic Compute Cloud (EC2), you don't even need hardware to get a site up and going in no time. You can literally go from nothing to a fully functional LAMP stack (operating system, web server, database, and programming language) and a free content management system (Drupal, for example) in less than a day. Sure, there are some things that are still quite time-consuming and complicated (writing software from scratch), but many of the basic services are easy and fast.

02 TECHNOLOGY GETS EASIER ALL THE TIME. I recall a time not all that long ago when installing software on Unix was a royal pain. You would download the release, then configure it, then compile it. And if you hadn't already installed required software dependencies (other applications the program needs), then you'd have to do those first. Today, installing applications and dependencies can be as simple as a one-line command (such as "sudo apt-get install X"). Plus, there are now projects like Bitnami that have prepackaged stacks that can take you from scratch to fully functional in a variety of applications in no time at all.

03 TECHNOLOGY GETS CHEAPER ALL THE TIME. I have rented a server from the same service provider for years. Recently when I filled my disk drive, I realized that I could pay the same amount per month but upgrade to a server with twice the RAM and more than twice the amount of disk space. Just keep breathing and what you can buy for the same amount of money gets better all the time.

04 MAXIMIZE THE EFFECTIVENESS OF YOUR MOST COSTLY TECHNOLOGY INVESTMENT—YOUR PEOPLE. As technology itself falls in price per unit, your staff is likely to get more expensive. So pay attention to what is required to make the most effective use of them. This means getting them the training and resources they need to do their job well. I can't believe how many administrators skimp on hardware and make their staff make do with inadequate amounts of RAM and processors when they are the least expensive part of the equation. Believe me, you do not want your most expensive resource sitting around waiting for your least expensive resource to boot up.

05 ITERATE, DON'T PERFECT. Librarians love perfection. We don't want to put any technology out for the public to use until we think it is perfect. Well, we need to get over ourselves. Savvy tech companies know the path to success is to *release early and iterate often*. One of the major benefits of this is that your users can provide early feedback on what they like and don't like, thereby providing essential input into further development. Do not be afraid of a beta or prototype label—people are now accustomed to such, and it can provide the necessary cover for being less than perfect.

06 BE PREPARED TO FAIL. Just as the pursuit of perfection is the enemy of progress, so is our fear of failure. Innovative organizations know that they will throw many things against the wall and only some will stick. But you don't usually know ahead of time which ones they will be, so you need to experiment, try things out, and see what works. This means you must be prepared for some experiments to fail. Just learn what you can and move on.

07 BE PREPARED TO SUCCEED. Hardly any technological success can be truly successful without a set of associated nontechnical efforts to support it. Full administrative support that is communicated throughout the organization is essential. Publicity is often key, to alert your user community to a new website or tool. Don't make the mistake of implementing a technology well but failing to get it out the door properly.

08 NEVER UNDERESTIMATE THE POWER OF A PROTOTYPE.
Prototypes are simple implementations of a new site or service that can demonstrate what a fully developed site or service would be like. Since many of us find it difficult to imagine a new site or service from a text description, prototypes can spark understanding in a way that few things can. Also, they tend to be much easier and faster to put together and can provide enough learning opportunities so that if you decide to support full development, the result will be more effective than it would have been otherwise.

09 A MAJOR PART OF GOOD TECHNOLOGY IMPLEMENTATION IS GOOD PROJECT MANAGEMENT. Many technology projects are not as simple as just installing an application—often the process is a long and complicated one that requires developing an implementation plan, a schedule, and collaboration with other individuals and departments. Therefore, many projects require good management to be successful. Keep in mind that your best technologist may not be your best project manager—this is why using teams is often the best implementation strategy for anything beyond minor projects.

10 THE SINGLE BIGGEST THREAT TO ANY TECHNOLOGY PROJECT IS POLITICAL IN NATURE. In the end, technology is the easy part. What's difficult is the people part. That's why your role, as library administrator, is the single most important in any implementation. Are you willing to throw your political support behind it? Are you willing to invest the resources required to make it a success? Will you marshal the entire organization to support, promote, and use this new site or service? If not, simply don't bother. If yes, then welcome to what will likely be a successful project.

LEIGH ANNE VRABEL'S 10 THINGS TO DO WHEN YOU ARE A LIBRARY DIRECTOR

LEIGH ANNE VRABEL, senior librarian for reference services at the Carnegie Library of Pittsburgh, has vowed to become a library director some day, and she has some good ideas about the kind of administrator she wants to be. She writes: "I spend a good chunk of my time thinking about that goal, and how I will get there. The result of all that thinking is this somewhat idealistic list of things I solemnly swear I will do when I am a library director. Those of you who currently wear that hat may smile or correct me as you please, but these are my thoughts based on my perspective in the here and now."

01 I WILL KNOW THE FIRST AND LAST NAMES OF EVERYBODY I WORK WITH. Yes, even if it's a big library. Yes, from the person who cleans the toilets to the president of my board. I will take an active, genuine interest in their lives, seeing them not merely as employees but as people with hopes and dreams who, properly cultivated, can make the organization a better place through their personal growth and development.

02 I WILL TREAT EVERYONE ON MY STAFF WITH DIGNITY AND RESPECT. If I am wrong, I will apologize. If I must do something unpopular, I will clearly explain why. I will communicate with them frequently and respect everyone's inherent worth, regardless of race, religion, gender, class, or favorite sports team.

03 I WILL NURTURE AND ENCOURAGE INNOVATION AND CHANGE. I will support my staff when they have wild and crazy ideas, give them the opportunity to test out their theories, even—perhaps especially—those about which I am skeptical. I will trust that they love the library and the community and that they have its best interests at heart. I will actively seek out staff and volunteers who can help me create a twenty-first-century library for twenty-first-century patron needs, and I will be fearless about trying new things and making mistakes.

I WILL PITCH IN AND HELP WITH WHATEVER TASK NEEDS TO BE DONE, NO MATTER HOW BIG OR SMALL. One thing that left a big impression on me as an undergraduate was an event the college president organized every year during homecoming. He called it "Lance Cooks," and it means exactly what it says: He cooked and served food in the cafeteria line and made conversation with everybody who passed through. It blew my mind that the college president would do that, and it made me feel good about the future of our campus. It also makes me want to be the director who opens the front doors every morning or who works the circulation desk regularly.

 I WILL LIVE IN THE COMMUNITY I SERVE AND BECOME AN ACTIVE, ENGAGED MEMBER OF IT. No ridiculous commutes for me. I want to be up close to the action, shopping in the community's stores, volunteering at its other nonprofits, and getting to know its people in all sorts of situations, not just director-patron ones. If my job is to lead a library, then I want to do it in the most accessible fashion possible. The title of director should be a bridge, not a barrier.

06 **I WILL DRESS UP LIKE A PIRATE ON HALLOWEEN.** Okay, to be fair, I'm already planning on doing that anyway—but that's not the point! Leadership is a serious business, especially during difficult times. However, I don't ever want to lose sight of the fact that, despite its difficulties, life has plenty of fun things to offer, and I will strive to create an atmosphere of fun, trust, and bonhomie in my library.

07 **I WILL BEND OVER BACKWARDS TO MAKE THE ARCANA OF LIBRARIANSHIP TRANSPARENT AND COMPREHENSIBLE TO MY BOARD.** Face it: There will always be some issue that only librarians care about, and it will make trustees' eyes glaze over if we try to explain it to them, no matter how much we prettify the language. That said, we *are* degree-holding professionals with particular skill sets and rationales for why we do things. Sometimes we need to explain this to a board—cheerfully and with patience. This is my area of least expertise, but I have served on one strategic-planning committee and gotten a good introduction to the scope of the task.

08 I WILL BE A LOUD, AGGRESSIVE, PASSIONATE, FEARLESS ADVOCATE FOR LIBRARIES. I will blog. I will write collection development policies that uphold the community's freedom to read. I will podcast. I will take advantage of every traditional and emerging technology to get the word out about the value of my library. I will cultivate relationships with my state and U.S. senators and representatives. I will work with my Friends group. I will get deeply involved at all levels of library advocacy.

09 I WILL EMBRACE TRANSPARENCY WHENEVER POSSIBLE. I will make it easy for community members to contact me. I will have an open-door policy with the staff. I will hold open houses and community meetings, and I will communicate early and often about any service changes that might come along. I will be candid about library finances. I will ensure, whether or not I'm actually responsible for its maintenance, that my library's website contains the most up-to-date information about the library, its policies and procedures, and its resources.

10 I WILL STAY HUMBLE, GROUNDED, AND FOCUSED. I will constantly question whether or not the actions I take are in the best interests of my staff and the community. I will earn my salary with blood, sweat, and tears, down to the last penny. I will surround myself with intelligent people who will gently but firmly correct me if I am drifting off course. I will network with other library directors and learn from their expertise, not just when I'm a newbie, but for as long as I have the privilege to lead. I will aggressively pursue continuing education opportunities, and my default setting will be that there is always, *always* something more to learn. Finally, I will be open to the lessons in all life experiences, including the gut-wrenching, painful ones.

JENNY LEVINE'S MIND-SET LIST FOR LIBRARY SCHOOL STUDENTS

EVERY YEAR SINCE 1998, humanities professor Tom McBride of Beloit College, Wisconsin, has produced a Beloit College Mindset List, which reminds teachers and administrators that the worldview of incoming freshmen is completely different from their own or even that of students from previous years. Jenny Levine, ALA's strategy guide, has created her own list that focuses on the information mind-set of students entering graduate library and information studies in 2010.

Jenny explains how she came up with the idea: "It's helpful for me to have reminders that my view of the world is shaped by different forces than those who come after me. Logically I know these things, but the Beloit Mindset List always brings these thoughts to the forefront when I read that for incoming freshmen: There have always been flat-screen TVs, tattoos have always been accepted and highly visible, and library catalogs never had cards. So this got me thinking about what a Beloit Mindset List would be for incoming library school students. If you're like me and you graduated from library school in the last century, this is a great jumping-off point for thinking about specific behaviors (and changes in behavior) that affect things like the reference interview, information foraging, and search boxes."

 Their cell phones have always let them access information, not just people, wherever they are.

 Video games have always been a social activity.

 They have always had to narrow down search results (rather than expand them).

 They have always used a different medium to communicate with their friends than with adults.

 They may never need to write a check. (I don't think I need the "may," but just in case.)

 They think of communication in 160-character chunks.

Their default
expectation is
wireless access.

 They have
never started
a search at an
"advanced"
screen.

 They store
information
and docu-
ments on key
chains.

 They have always
copied and pasted.

 The symbol "." is
pronounced "dot," not
"period."

 Content creation has always been
instantaneous (take a picture and see it,
start typing to create a document and save it,
type a status update and hit Enter).

 Applications are something they use, not something they fill out.

 They carry their music collections in the palms of their hands,
although soon they will access music from anywhere through their
cell phones.

They are the only generation to grow up with DVDs, the last to grow
up with physical media.

SEAN FITZPATRICK'S 7 COOL TOOLS THAT LIBRARIANS SHOULD KNOW ABOUT

AMERICAN LIBRARIES ASSOCIATE EDITOR Sean Fitzpatrick is the mastermind behind *AL*'s new Drupal-based website. He is always experimenting with apps to make our work easier and make us seem trendy. Here's what he says: "There's no shortage of really cool tools and apps to download, install, and play with. Some of it is pure fun, but many programs can help make us more productive, better connected, and more efficient at work. Here are some of the top tools. They're all free, and many are open source."

01 LIBRARYH3LP (http://libraryh3lp.com). LibraryH3lp is an integrated web chat and instant messaging platform written specifically for libraries. It allows multiple librarians to receive chats from its native chat widget or meebo me! widgets, as well as IMs from patrons on other networks. Unlike meebo me!, LibraryH3lp's chat widget is not Flash-based, which means it's usable on mobile devices and your patrons won't need up-to-date Flash on their end. You get started by registering, which creates your top-level admin account, then use the account to create other users, queues, and IM gateways and to work with the system.

02 TEAMVIEWER (http://teamviewer.com). This super-simple screen-sharing app lets you collaborate on projects, troubleshoot remote PCs, gain access to remote computers in a way similar to a virtual private network, or run ad hoc webinars and meetings. The software establishes connections to any PC or server around the world within just a few seconds. You don't need admin privileges to use it, and it seems to work through most firewalls. Just download, install, run, and tell the person you're sharing with to do the same.

03 GOOGLE WAVE (http://wave.google.com). Librarians go gaga over Google for many reasons. Google has changed the way we search, Google Docs has changed the way we create and share documents and forms, Google Sites has made tracking reference-desk stats a lot easier, Google Scholar gives patrons one interface to search many scholarly database indexes at once, Google Reader is hands-down the best RSS reader I've seen, and the list goes on. But the one tool that trumps the rest—even though at the time I am writing this, I've only had a beta account for a few days—is Wave. Google Wave combines functions of e-mail, IM, online forums, document sharing, and all kinds of multimedia support into a totally new communication protocol that even at first glance proves to be much more than the sum of its parts. The only way to figure out how you can make use of it is to get it and experiment with it.

04 SCREENGRAB (www.screengrab.org). Screengrab is a Firefox add-on that saves web pages as images, without the need to hit Print Screen. It captures what you can see in the window—the entire page, just a selection, or a particular frame—and lets you save it as a PNG file or copy it to the clipboard. Need to edit those screenshots too? Try Aviary (http://aviary.com), which adds web-based image-editing capabilities to its screen-capture add-on.

05 VDOWNLOADER (http://vdownloader.es). Most of the time, the YouTube videos we really like seem to stick around. We just have faith they'll be there when we want them. But what about those times when the librarian inside us says we should be saving them, archiving them for the future? In steps VDownloader, a simple tool that can download and convert videos from all the major sites, including YouTube, Vimeo, Blip TV, Google Video, Yahoo! Video, and lots more.

06 PORTABLE APPS SUITE (http://portableapps.com). It's not uncommon for librarians to work with several different computers every day: a back-office machine, one at the reference desk, one or two at home, a laptop for conferences. Switching between them can be a pain. The Portable Apps Suite, a host of software applications that runs on your USB drive, makes life a lot simpler. Portable Apps has Firefox, Pidgin IM, Thunderbird mail client, and Open Office, among others, and they run on any computer, anywhere. It even has a couple of games— because working nights at the reference desk can get lonely.

07 FIREBUG (http://getfirebug.com). If you're like me, you're not technically a web developer, but you took a class about it in library school and you now like to dabble. The Firebug add-on for Firefox lets you easily learn about what's going on behind the scenes on any website by showing you the HTML, CSS, and JavaScript code for any section of the site as you roll the mouse pointer around the page. Firebug is great for troubleshooting your own sites or for snooping around the back end of any site on the Web, without having to "view source."

KEY DATES IN AMERICAN LIBRARY HISTORY

1638 Upon his death, the Rev. John Harvard bequeaths £779 and a library of some 400 volumes to the New College founded in Cambridge, Massachusetts, in 1636, which becomes Harvard College in 1639. A fire destroys Old Harvard Hall on January 24, 1764, consuming all the books in the original collection except one, *The Christian Warfare Against the Deuill, World, and Flesh* by John Downame, which had been checked out by a student.

1731 Benjamin Franklin founds the Library Company of Philadelphia as the first subscription library supported by members. Prominent citizens can buy stock in the company in order to become a member and borrow books.

1743 The Darby (Pa.) Library Company is founded by a group of Quakers for the use of subscribing members only. Only later will it become a free library funded by public tax support, the Darby Free Library. The library's current building was erected in 1872.

1747 The Redwood Library and Athenaeum in Newport, Rhode Island, is established by Abraham Redwood and a group of his friends and associates with 751 books. A private subscription library, it is the oldest community library still occupying its original building.

1762 William Rind, a bookseller of Annapolis, Maryland, starts up the first circulating library in America. He loans out two books at a time for those willing to pay a moderate fee, but the scheme is not successful and collapses by 1764.

1815 Congress purchases Thomas Jefferson's library of nearly 6,500 books to replace the collection lost when the British Army burned the Capitol in 1814 during the War of 1812. It forms the basis of the new Library of Congress.

1827 A municipally supported juvenile library opens in Lexington, Massachusetts.

1833 The Peterborough (N.H.) Town Library is established. It is the first institution founded by a municipality with the explicit purpose of establishing a free library open to all classes of the community and supported by public funds.

1848 The Boston Public Library, the first large, free municipal library in the United States, is founded by an act of the Great and General Court of Massachusetts.

1849 The state of New Hampshire passes the first general free public library law in the United States.

1851 The first Young Men's Christian Association library is set up in Boston.

1862 Harvard librarian John Langdon Sibley creates a public card catalog using cards that measure 2 inches by 5 inches, stored in a cabinet designed by his assistant, Ezra Abbott.

1876 Melvil Dewey copyrights his decimal classification system and founds the Library Bureau company in Boston. The American Library Association is founded and meets for the first time in Philadelphia, October 4–6.

1882 Caroline Hewins initiates the story hour at the Hartford (Conn.) Young Men's Institute, a private subscription association that is the predecessor to the Hartford Public Library.

 1887 Melvil Dewey establishes the first formal school for library education, the School of Library Economy, at Columbia University.

 1888 The first children's room in an American public library is established on the third floor of the George Bruce Library at 226 W. 42nd Street in New York City.

1889 The first library in the United States built with funds granted by philanthropist and steel magnate Andrew Carnegie is dedicated in Braddock, Pennsylvania, and is at first intended to serve employees of his first major steel mill, the Edgar Thomson Works, and their families. A year later, Carnegie dedicates the first tax-supported U.S. public library, the Carnegie Free Library of Allegheny, Pennsylvania. He goes on to fund the construction of more than 2,500 libraries in the United States, Canada, Great Britain, Ireland, Australia, New Zealand, Serbia, the Caribbean, and Fiji for the next 40 years.

 1890 Cleveland Public Library becomes the first large public library to adopt an unrestricted open access policy.

 1898 The first course devoted to children's librarianship is established at the New York State Library School in Albany.

 1901 The Library of Congress begins the sale and distribution of pre-printed catalog cards to libraries throughout the United States.

 1903 Charles Martel completes the outline of a system of 21 subject classes that forms the basis of the Library of Congress classification system.

 1904 The first structure built specifically to offer public library service to African Americans opens in Henderson, Kentucky, at the rear of the Eighth Street Colored School.

 1905 The Washington County (Md.) Free Library in Hagerstown launches the first bookmobile as a horse-drawn book wagon designed by Library Director Mary Lemist Titcomb.

1906 The first master's degree in library science is conferred at the New York State Library School in Albany.

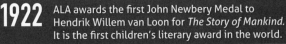 **1922** ALA awards the first John Newbery Medal to Hendrik Willem van Loon for *The Story of Mankind.* It is the first children's literary award in the world.

 1923 The Springfield (Mass.) Public Library is one of the first U.S. libraries to circulate music recordings.

 1926 The Graduate Library School is established at the University of Chicago. It becomes the first to enroll doctoral students in librarianship in 1928.

 1939 ALA adopts the Library Bill of Rights, originally written by Forrest Spaulding, director of the Des Moines (Iowa) Public Library, in 1938.

 1947 The Public Library Inquiry, the first national assessment of the status of public libraries and librarians in the United States, is initiated by ALA and the Carnegie Corporation.

 1950 The first drive-through service windows are established for book returns at the Cincinnati Public Library.

 1956 Congress passes the Library Services Act, allowing for federal funding of public libraries.

 1958 The first National Library Week is celebrated May 16–22, with the theme "Wake Up and Read!"

 1960 The first civil rights sit-in at a library takes place in the Petersburg (Va.) Public Library and results in the arrest of 11 black students for trespassing.

 1964 One of the first electronic theft detection systems is installed at the Grand Rapids (Mich.) Public Library.

1970 Ohio State University launches one of the first campuswide online public access catalogs with its IBM-developed Library Control System.

1972 Stanford University's BALLOTS is the earliest successful implementation of an integrated library system.

 1981 ALA's Banned Books Week begins as a celebration of the freedom to read.

 1982 The national library symbol debuts at the ALA Annual Conference in Philadelphia as a way for libraries to promote awareness of their services.

 1987 ALA and the National Commission on Libraries launch the first Library Card Sign-up Month as part of a national campaign to combat illiteracy. Hundreds of thousands of children and adults receive library cards during the first year of the campaign.

 1996 The Institute of Museum and Library Services is established by Congress as the main source of federal support for libraries and museums.

 1998 The ALA Young Adult Library Services Association holds the first Teen Read Week in October.

 1999 Rockefeller University Library in New York City and Farmington (Mich.) Community Library are the first to use RFID chips to circulate materials.

 2006 ALA launches the weekly e-newsletter *American Libraries Direct*.

 2009 Anythink Brighton, a branch of the Rangeview Library District in Adams County, Colorado, becomes the first carbon-positive library in the United States, offsetting 16 percent more carbon than it uses.

5 MOVIES WITH THE WORST LIBRARIAN STEREOTYPES

01 *CHAINSAW SALLY* (2004). Drab Porterville librarian Sally Diamon (played by April Monique Burril) turns into an insane, cannibalistic, chainsaw-slinging, goth vigilante at night, dealing death to those who threaten her or her cross-dressing brother. She offs one male patron in the library men's room for being noisy, and brutally executes Tina in the woods for not returning the overdue *Atkins for Life* diet book.

02 *IT'S A WONDERFUL LIFE* (1946). George Bailey (played by Jimmy Stewart) becomes so depressed on Christmas Eve that he wishes he had never been born. To turn him around, his guardian angel Clarence offers him a glimpse of what the world would have been like without him. Deprived of the chance to become his attractive, vivacious wife, Mary (played by Donna Reed) instead is destined for spinsterhood and a career as a (gasp) nearsighted, dowdy, panicky librarian.

03 *THE MUSIC MAN* (1962). Shirley Jones as Marian (the librarian) Paroo tries to expose Robert Preston as a con man: "Professor Harold Hill, Gary Conservatory of Music, class of '05. Harold, there wasn't any Gary Conservatory of Music in '05. . . . The town wasn't even built until '06." But she is prudish, slams library books around, tears pages out of journals, wields a rubber stamp like a Soviet bureaucrat, is completely inept at handling problem patrons, and tries to interest the locals in Balzac and Chaucer when they would be better off with Mark Twain.

04 *THE NAME OF THE ROSE* (1986). Volker Prechtel is Malachia, the librarian of a Benedictine abbey in northern Italy in 1327 and a conspirator in the plot to keep secret the existence of a copy of Aristotle's lost second book of *Poetics,* which deals with comedic verse. Because the monks believe that laughter is a Satanic distraction, they keep the book sequestered in the library's labyrinthine tower (violating Ranganathan's "Books are for use" law), and one of them has poisoned the pages, causing the deaths of several sneaky readers, including Malachia himself.

05 *SOPHIE'S CHOICE* (1982). Meryl Streep as Sophie Zawistowska, a Polish immigrant, seeks a book by the American poet Emily Dickinson, but she mispronounces it "Emil Dickens." A prissy, surly male New York librarian played by John Rothman assumes the role of poster child for Worst Reference Interview and tells her to go to the card catalog, even though she won't find anything. "Everyone knows," he oozes, "that Charles Dickens was an English writer. There is no American poet by the name of Dickens." Sophie is so taken aback by his deskside manner that she faints.

5 MOVIES WITH LIBRARIAN ROLE MODELS

01 *DESK SET* (1957). A group of information specialists (played by Katharine Hepburn, Joan Blondell, Dina Merrill, and Sue Randall) at a television network are confronted with automation when efficiency expert Spencer Tracy arrives to install a new computer called EMMARAC (Electromagnetic Memory and Research Arithmetical Calculator). It turns out that their jobs are not really at risk, but it gives them a chance to demonstrate that technology is a tool, not a replacement for human expertise.

02 *THE GUN IN BETTY LOU'S HANDBAG* (1992). Penelope Ann Miller plays a children's librarian in Missouri named Betty Lou Perkins, who falsely confesses to murder to get the attention of her policeman husband (okay, not role model material, but she wants to improve her mousy image). She likes books, has creative ideas, and tries to get people excited about what the library does. At her trial, the judge says, "That's Betty Lou Perkins? Hell, I don't go to the library enough." The fund-raiser scene is a good advocacy statement for libraries.

03 *THE SHAWSHANK REDEMPTION* (1994). Tim Robbins as model prisoner Andy Dufresne befriends the old Shawshank Prison librarian (who calls his library job "Easy peasy Japanesey") and transforms the library into a well-stocked collection over the next 23 years. He offers high-school-equivalency educational programs, opera-appreciation day, and tax services for prison officials.

04 *STORM CENTER* (1956). Bette Davis plays Alicia Hull, a small-town public librarian who refuses to remove a book on communism from the shelves, an action the city fathers have made a prerequisite for granting funds for a children's wing. At the town meeting, a local attorney accuses her of being a Communist herself and turns the citizens against her, ultimately undermining the loyalty of a young patron who burns the library down. The screenplay was loosely based on Ruth Brown, librarian at the Bartlesville (Okla.) Public Library, who was fired in 1950, ostensibly for having subversive books in the library, but in reality for her civil rights activism in the 1940s. Her story is detailed in Louise S. Robbins's *The Dismissal of Miss Ruth Brown: Civil Rights, Censorship, and the American Library* (University of Oklahoma Press, 2000).

05 *THE MUMMY* (1999). Rachel Weisz plays Evelyn Cameron, a young Egyptologist and librarian in Cairo in the 1920s. Her drunken declaration, "I may not be an explorer or an adventurer or a treasure seeker or a gunfighter, Mr. O'Connell, but I am proud of what I am. I . . . am . . . a librarian!" is inspirational. In an early scene, she manages to topple all the shelving in a library ("Oops!"), but it is her linguistic skill and knowledge that help the seekers find the lost city of Hamunaptra.

3 TV SHOWS WITH LIBRARIANS

01 *BUFFY THE VAMPIRE SLAYER* (1997–2003). Anthony Stewart Head plays Rupert Giles, the librarian at Sunnydale (Calif.) High School, who as a Watcher is responsible for the care and training of the Slayer. The school library, which serves as the unofficial command center for Buffy's slayage activities, happens to be situated atop the Hellmouth, a conduit for paranormal activity. Giles's technophobia, his mastery of occult books and arcane lore, and his British stuffiness were all part of the show's comedic success. Some Giles quotes:

> "Once again, I teeter on the precipice of the generation gap."
> "I'm sure my books and I are in for a fascinating afternoon."
> "She lives very much in the now, and well, history is very
>   much about the then."
> *Buffy:* "Lie to me." *Giles:* "Yes, it's terribly simple. The good
>   guys are always stalwart and true. The bad guys are eas-
>   ily distinguished by the pointy horns or black hats. And,
>   uh, we always defeat them and save the day. No one ever
>   dies, and everybody lives happily ever after." *Buffy:* "Liar."

02 *THE LIBRARIANS* (2007–). Frances O'Brien (played by series cocre-ator Robyn Butler), a devout Catholic and panic-disorder sufferer, runs a tight ship as head librarian at the Middleton Interactive Learning Centre, a suburban public library, in this Australian comedy. Her life unravels when she is forced to employ her ex-best friend, Christine Grimwood—now facing criminal drug charges—as the children's librarian. As pointed out by director Wayne Hope, the variety of peo-ple at a public library makes it ripe for comedy material. The series does not shy away from unusual topics, including multicultural ten-sions, dyslexia, a paraplegic staff member, and even an accreditation hearing. The Australian Library and Information Association launched a blog (www.alia.org.au/thelibrariansblog/) to serve as a professional forum about the show. A second season aired in 2009, and Butler and Hope announced plans to bring the series to the United States.

03 *TWILIGHT ZONE* (June 2, 1961), "The Obsolete Man." In a totalitarian State that has made literacy a crime, librarian Romney Wordsworth (played by Burgess Meredith) is considered obsolete. The prosecuting Chancellor declares that there are no longer any books, and therefore no need for a librarian. Wordsworth is sentenced to die, but he cleverly sets a trap to demonstrate that the individual is stronger than the State.

In another episode, "Time Enough at Last" (aired November 20, 1959), Burgess Meredith plays a bookish bank teller who survives a nuclear holocaust. He discovers that the public library's collection is intact, and he begins a plan of uninterrupted reading for years to come. Just as he settles down to read, his glasses slip from his face and shatter. The episode ends as he cries, "That's not fair at all. There was time now. There was all the time I needed! *It's not fair!*"

12 LIBRARIANS WHO CAME BACK TO HAUNT

MANY AMERICAN LIBRARIES are said to be haunted, but only a few harbor ghosts that can be linked to former custodians of the collection. Do some librarians return from the dead to wander the stacks again? I don't know. Perhaps the books in bibliothèques soak up enough of our energies to generate a frisson of fantasy long after we are gone. At any rate, here are a dozen cases of postmortem persistence, all in libraries.

01 LYDIA BARTON, director of the Clapp Memorial Library, Belchertown, Massachusetts, 1887–1911. In 2007, night custodian Jacques J. Benoit reported apparitions moving up and down the stairs, cold spots, and books sliding in and out of the shelves. When he heard an unexplained noise, he said out loud, "It's OK, Lydia," and the noise stopped.

02 EDUARD BERTZ (1853–1931), German radical socialist refugee and librarian who organized the collection of the Thomas Hughes Memorial Library, Historic Rugby, Tennessee, from 1881 to 1883. Bertz is said to have appeared to Brian Stagg in the late 1960s and provided hints on how to restore the library to its original shelf arrangement.

03 RUTH COCHRAN, assistant librarian, Umatilla County Public Library, Pendleton, Oregon. Cochran suffered a cerebral hemorrhage while she was closing the building October 11, 1947. She went to the basement to rest, but was found the next day and taken to the hospital, where she died. Spooky events were blamed on Ruth until the library moved to a new location in 1996. Once, a custodian was alone in the building painting the children's room when the intercom system buzzed repeatedly.

04 ALBERT J. EDMUNDS (1857–1941), cataloger, Historical Society of Pennsylvania, Philadelphia. A spectral typist frequently heard in a room on the third floor is said to be Edmunds.

05 AMELIA GAYLE GORGAS (1823–1913), university librarian at the University of Alabama, Tuscaloosa, 1879–1906. Completed in 1937, the Gorgas Library was named after her. Although the elevators can be locked so they don't stop on the fourth floor where the special collections are housed, one elevator stops there anyway, with no passengers on it. The elevator high jinks are attributed to Gorgas's ghost.

06 IDA DAY HOLZAPFEL, head librarian, Hutchinson (Kans.) Public Library, 1915–1925, 1947–1954. Her ghost has been seen and heard since her death in California in 1954. Library staffer Rose Hale said she saw a lady standing below the stairs one day. She did not know the woman's name, but when she described the woman to another library employee, Hale was told she had just described Ida Day. Other employees claim to have heard footsteps in the basement, and it became a shared joke that whenever anything was misplaced or missing, Ida Day took it.

07 ETHEL MCDOWELL, director of the Ashtabula County (Ohio) District Library, 1903–1968, is said to have haunted the library prior to an October 1991 fire that took place during a million-dollar renovation. Odd footsteps were heard in the second-floor storage area, and apparitions and cold spots were reported in the basement hallway.

08 CATHARINE MCMURCHY, director of the Snohomish (Wash.) Carnegie Library, 1923–1939. McMurchy died in 1956, and her ghost could be seen or heard walking in the basement of this 1910 Carnegie before the library moved to modern quarters in 2003. In 1991, children's librarian Debbie Young was taking a break in the staff room when she saw an older woman walk down the stairs from a storage area and exit the room. For a while the library had a ghostcam to try to catch her appearances, the last of which may have occurred the night of November 9, 2002, according to the *Everett Herald* of January 24, 2003 (although it could have been a janitorial service worker).

09 ANGE V. MILNER (1856–1928), library director, Illinois State University, Normal. Milner's ghost was allegedly seen by several faculty, staff, and students in the Williams Hall library. Archives specialist Jo Rayfield sensed a "kind, gentle" presence one day while looking at microfilm. Others have reported cold spots, a white figure, and books restacked in an odd fashion. Williams Hall was retired as a library after the construction of the new Milner Library (named after Ange) in 1976.

10 GEORGE F. SANBORN,. first librarian of the Meredith (N.H.) Public Library, established in 1882. A psychic who investigated the library in August 2008 said she communicated with a spirit that matched Sanborn's description.

11 FANT THORNLEY,. director of the Birmingham (Ala.) Public Library, 1953–1970. People have reported strange sensations, objects moved, and a spirit that occasionally sneaks a smoke. Thornley used to enjoy Chesterfields. The third-floor auditorium is a favorite hangout.

12 ELLEN SUMMERS WILSON,. first director of the Public Library of Steubenville and Jefferson County, Ohio, 1902–1904. Her office was located in the central tower, and after she died in 1904 stories began to circulate about creaking sounds and footsteps in the unoccupied attic. Today the attic houses air conditioning equipment that mysteriously turned itself off—until the controls were moved downstairs.

TOP **15** BOOKS ABOUT REAL LIBRARIANS

01 JANE BRODSKY FITZPATRICK, *Mrs. Magavero: A History Based on the Career of an Academic Librarian* (Duluth, Minn.: Library Juice Press, 2007). Filomena Magavero worked at the Stephen B. Luce Library at SUNY Maritime College in the Bronx from 1949 to 2003. Until 1965, she was the only female staff member on campus. The book includes an oral history that offers a glimpse of what it was like to be a library worker in the prefeminist era.

02 MARILYN JOHNSON, *This Book Is Overdue! How Librarians and Cybrarians Can Save Us All* (New York: HarperCollins, 2010). Johnson—a former staff writer for *Life* and editor at *Esquire, Redbook,* and *Outside*—writes about contemporary librarians as visionaries, technologists, information experts, and advocates of literacy, open access, and the freedom to read.

03 FRANK KINGDON, *John Cotton Dana: A Life* (Newark, N.J.: Newark Public Library and Museum, 1940). This tribute to John Cotton Dana (1856–1929) follows his career from childhood in Vermont to his library work in Denver, Springfield (Massachusetts), and Newark. Dana's humor and commitment to the library as part of the life of a community often turn up in his writings; for example, he wrote: "I believe there is more inspiration to civic decency for a child in the story of how the community gets a supply of pure water than there is in the best fairy tale ever devised or the noblest Teutonic myth ever born."

04 KENNETH F. KISTER, *Eric Moon: The Life and Library Times* (Jefferson, N.C.: McFarland, 2002). British-born librarian Eric Moon (b. 1923) was editor of *Library Journal* from 1959 to 1968 and has been a major influence on the profession's advocacy of civil rights, intellectual freedom, and social responsibility. This bio portrays him as a twentieth-century Melvil Dewey.

KATHRYN LASKY. *The Librarian Who Measured the Earth* (Boston: Joy Street Books, 1994). Eratosthenes was the third scholar placed in charge of the great Library of Alexandria, Egypt, from ca. 246 BC to ca. 195 BC. He was also the first person to calculate the circumference of the earth with any accuracy (off only by 1 percent). This picture book also gives kids an idea of what ancient libraries were like.

ROSALEE MCREYNOLDS AND LOUISE S. ROBBINS. *The Librarian Spies: Philip and Mary Jane Keeney and Cold War Espionage* (Westport, Conn.: Praeger, 2009). McReynolds and Robbins tell the little-known story of Philip Olin Keeney (1891–1962) and his wife Mary Jane (1898–1969) who were allegedly part of the Silvermaster spy ring that passed information to the Soviets in the 1940s. Outspoken leftists and freedom of information advocates since their days at the University of Montana in the 1930s and their role in founding the Progressive Librarians Council in 1939, they were brought before the House Un-American Activities Committee in 1949, which effectively ruined their careers.

EDWARD JOHN MILLER. *Prince of Librarians: Life and Times of Antonio Panizzi of the British Museum* (London: Deutsch, 1967). A life of Italian political exile Anthony Panizzi (1797–1879) who escaped to England in 1823 and enjoyed a long career at the British Library as assistant librarian (1831–1837), keeper of printed books (1837–1856), and chief librarian (1856–1866). His sketch for a new reading room led to the construction of the famed circular reading room in use from 1857 to 1997.

VICKI MYRON. *Dewey: The Small-Town Library Cat Who Touched the World* (New York: Grand Central, 2008). Dewey Readmore Books was the cat who lived at the Spencer (Iowa) Public Library and served as its patron greeter and de facto public-relations ambassador from 1988 to 2006. Although much of the book concerns Dewey, who turned up in the library's book drop one frigid January morning, it's also about the people of Spencer, especially Myron (Spencer's former library director) who realized Dewey's potential to transform the community's perception of the library.

JOANNE ELLEN PASSET. *Cultural Crusaders: Women Librarians in the American West, 1900–1917* (Albuquerque: University of New Mexico, 1994). This is an overview of the lives of several hundred women who participated in the development of libraries in the American West during the first two decades of the twentieth century. A final chapter presents brief biographies of four representative librarians—

Ida Angeline Clarke Kidder (Oregon State University), Mary Frances Isom (Multnomah County Library), Charlotte A. Baker (Denver Public Library), and Mary Belle Sweet (University of Idaho).

10 JANE AIKIN ROSENBERG. *The Nation's Great Library: Herbert Putnam and the Library of Congress, 1899–1939* (Urbana: University of Illinois, 1993). Herbert Putnam (1861–1955) was the first experienced librarian to head the Library of Congress. With his expertise in organization and his desire to create a national library, Putnam transformed LC into a major cultural institution that set the parameters for American library development. He also created the world's first national catalog card service.

11 FRANCES CLARK SAYERS. *Anne Carroll Moore: A Biography* (New York: Atheneum, 1972). Anne Carroll Moore (1871–1961) headed the Children's Department of the Pratt Institute Free Library in Brooklyn from 1896 to 1906 and was the first supervisor of work with children at the New York Public Library from 1906 to 1941. In this position Moore hired and trained children's librarians, oversaw book purchases, and planned children's rooms for many of the library's branches. Moore was also the librarian who befriended Leo Frank, a Jewish factory manager in Atlanta wrongly (it turned out) convicted for the murder of thirteen-year-old Mary Phagan and lynched by a mob in 1915. He had been a regular visitor to the Pratt children's library in his youth.

12 BARRY W. SEAVER. *A True Politician: Rebecca Browning Rankin, Municipal Reference Librarian of the City of New York, 1920–1952* (Jefferson, N.C.: McFarland, 2003). During the Depression, Rankin teamed with Mayor Fiorello La Guardia and other library officials to provide pensions for public librarians in New York City. They shared the belief that government should carry out the will of the people and care for their needs through intelligently planned services, and they worked together to make this belief a reality.

13 PAT WALSH. *The Curious Case of the Mayo Librarian* (Cork, Ireland: Mercier Press, 2009). In July 1930, the appointment of Trinity College graduate Letitia Dunbar Harrison (1906–1994) as librarian in Mayo County, Ireland, resulted in a full-scale political crisis. Local priests and politicians attempted to have her removed, ostensibly because her grasp of the Irish language was inadequate, but primarily because she was Protestant and not from the area. She accepted a transfer to another position after little more than a year.

14 WAYNE A. WIEGAND, *Irrepressible Reformer: A Biography of Melvil Dewey* (Chicago: American Library Association, 1996). Wiegand captures the essence of America's most famous librarian, warts and all. In addition to Dewey's well-known accomplishments in helping to found ALA in 1876, his Library Bureau business venture, his efforts at spelling reform, his pioneering leadership in library and adult education, and his development of the Dewey Decimal Classification, Wiegand covers the accusations of sexual harassment, anti-Semitism, arrogance, pugnacity, and duplicity that haunted Dewey throughout his career.

15 JEANETTE WINTER, *The Librarian of Basra: A True Story from Iraq* (Orlando, Fla.: Harcourt, 2005). Alia Muhammad Baker, director of the Central Library in Basra, Iraq, managed to save more than 30,000 volumes, about 70 percent of the collection, by storing them in homes just prior to the bombing by Anglo-American forces that destroyed the building in 2003. A nicely illustrated children's book that connects kids to recent world events.

12 LIBRARIANS WHO WERE POETS

 JOHN VANCE CHENEY (1848–1922), Newberry Library, Chicago, 1894–1899. *Queen Helen, and Other Poems* (Chicago: Way and Williams, 1895).

 SAM WALTER FOSS (1858–1911), Somerville (Mass.) Public Library, 1898–1911. *The Song of the Library Staff* (New York: J. R. Anderson, 1906).

 PHILIP LARKIN (1922–1985), University of Hull, United Kingdom, 1955–1985. *The Whitsun Weddings* (London: Faber and Faber, 1964).

04 **GOTTHOLD EPHRAIM LESSING** (1729–1781), Herzog August Bibliothek, Wolfenbüttel, Germany, 1770–1781. *Nathan der Weise: Ein dramatisches Gedicht* (n.p., 1779).

 AUDRE LORDE (1934–1992), Town School library, New York City, 1966–1968. *The First Cities* (New York: Poets Press, 1968).

06 **CHARLES FLETCHER LUMMIS** (1859–1928), Los Angeles Public Library, 1905–1910. *A Bronco Pegasus* (Boston: Houghton Mifflin, 1928).

07 ARCHIBALD MACLEISH (1892–1982), Library of Congress, 1939–1944. *Collected Poems, 1917–1982* (Boston: Houghton Mifflin, 1985).

08 CHRISTOPHER OKIGBO (1932–1967), University of Nigeria, Nsukka, 1960–1963. *Limits* (Ibadan, Nigeria: Mbari Publications, 1964).

09 MARY WRIGHT PLUMMER (1856–1916), Pratt Institute Free Library, Brooklyn, 1890–1911. *Verses* (Cleveland: De Vinne Press, 1896).

10 DUDLEY RANDALL (1914–2000), Wayne County (Mich.) Federated Library System, 1956–1969. *Poem Counterpoem* (Detroit: Broadside Press, 1966).

11 BRIGITTE RICHTER (1943–1991), La Médiathèque Louis Aragon, Le Mans, France. *Œuvres Poétiques* (Bernay, France: Édition Noë Richter, 1993).

12 WILLIAM FITCH SMYTH (1857–1940), Cleveland (Ohio) Public Library, 1904–1940. *Little Lyrics for Librarians* (Storrs, Conn.: University of Connecticut Library, 1974).

14 WAYS PUBLIC LIBRARIES ARE GOOD FOR THE COUNTRY

 01 LIBRARIES ENCOURAGE DEMOCRACY. Libraries provide access to information and multiple points of view so that citizens can make informed decisions on public policy.

 02 LIBRARIES BREAK DOWN BOUNDARIES. Libraries offer services and programs for people at all literacy levels, readers with little or no English skills, homebound senior citizens, prisoners, homeless or impoverished individuals, and persons with physical or learning disabilities.

 03 LIBRARIES LEVEL THE PLAYING FIELD. Libraries make their resources available to everyone in the community, regardless of income or social status.

 04 LIBRARIES VALUE INDEPENDENT THOUGHT. Libraries offer choices between mainstream and alternative viewpoints, between traditional and visionary concepts, and between monocultural and multicultural perspectives.

 05 LIBRARIES NOURISH CREATIVITY. By providing an atmosphere that stimulates curiosity, libraries create opportunities for unstructured learning and serendipitous discovery.

 06 LIBRARIES OFFER SANCTUARY. By providing an atmosphere conducive to reflection, libraries induce a feeling of serenity and transcendence that opens the mind to new ideas and interpretations.

07 LIBRARIES ANIMATE YOUNG MINDS. Children's and young adult librarians offer story hours, book talks, summer reading activities, career planning, art projects, gaming competitions, and other programs to spark youthful imaginations.

08 LIBRARIES EXTEND FAMILY ACTIVITIES. Libraries offer an alternate venue for parents and their children to enhance activities traditionally conducted at home by providing homework centers, parenting collections, after-school programs, outreach, one-on-one reading, and early literacy programs.

09 LIBRARIES BUILD TWENTY-FIRST-CENTURY SKILLS. Library services and programs foster critical-thinking skills, problem-solving aptitude, visual and scientific literacy, cross-disciplinary thinking, information and media literacy, productivity and leadership skills, civic literacy, global awareness, and health and environmental literacy.

10 LIBRARIES SERVE AS TECHNOLOGY HUBS. Libraries offer a wide range of public access computing and Internet access services at no charge to users. In 2009, more than 71 percent of U.S. libraries reported that they were the only provider of free computer and Internet access in their communities.

11 LIBRARIES OFFER A LIFELINE TO THE UNEMPLOYED. Library patrons search for jobs online, polish résumés with word processing software, fill out applications, research new professions, sign up for career workshops, and look for financial assistance.

12 LIBRARIES RETURN HIGH DIVIDENDS. Public libraries return to their communities anywhere from $1.30 to $10.00 in services for every $1.00 invested in them. In 2008, librarians delivered more than 409 million hours of service annually (197,000 U.S. librarians × 40 hours a week × 52 weeks). How valuable is your local library? Use the handy Library Value Calculator created by the Massachusetts Library Association (www.ilovelibraries.org/getinformed/getinvolved/calculator.cfm).

13 LIBRARIES BUILD COMMUNITIES. People gather at the library to find and share information, experience and experiment with the arts and media, and engage in community discussions and games.

14 LIBRARIES PRESERVE THE PAST. Libraries are repositories of community history, oral narratives, and audiovisual records of events and culture. When these local resources are digitized and placed online as digital libraries, communities and cultures 1,000 miles away can share in the experience.

RANGANATHAN'S 5 LAWS OF LIBRARY SCIENCE (UPDATED)

SHIYALI RAMAMRITA RANGANATHAN (1892–1972) was an Indian mathematician and librarian best known for his formulation of five guiding principles of librarianship. Because he originally drew these up in 1929, the laws are based on books as the primary building blocks of information. (However, he was enough of a futurist that in the 1950s he predicted the online catalog.) To bring Ranganathan's laws into the twenty-first century, I have added a brief interpretation.

01 BOOKS ARE FOR USE. Library users must be able to access information freely. Barriers to its use (poor user interfaces, prohibitive fees, limited hours of access, web content filters) should be eradicated or minimized.

02 EVERY PERSON HIS OR HER BOOK. Library users in a democratic society have the right to seek out, request, and obtain information for personal education or entertainment, regardless of race, gender, religion, age, ethnicity, language, political viewpoint, disability, or sexual preference.

03 EVERY BOOK, ITS READER. Libraries must create an environment that allows users to find not only the information or materials they need but also the information or materials they do not know they need.

04 SAVE THE TIME OF THE READER. Libraries must train and inspire their users to become information literate and thus lifelong learners. Library resources and services should be extended to users outside the library through such methods as online databases, distance education, digital reference, social networks, mobile libraries, and digital collections.

05 A LIBRARY IS A GROWING ORGANISM. Libraries must plan for the growth of their collections, the changing needs and demographics of their users, the expansion of staff skill sets, and the evolution of information technology.

MICHAEL GORMAN'S REVISED LAWS OF LIBRARY SCIENCE

MICHAEL GORMAN DEVELOPED these new laws of library science in the 1990s when he was dean of library services at California State University, Fresno.

 01 Libraries serve humanity.

 02 Respect all forms by which knowledge is communicated.

 03 Use technology intelligently to enhance service.

 04 Protect free access to knowledge.

 05 Honor the past and create the future.

JOHN COTTON DANA'S
12 RULES FOR READING

JOHN COTTON DANA (1856–1929) established one of the first children's rooms at the Denver Public Library in 1894 and was public library director in Springfield, Massachusetts, and Newark, New Jersey. He served as president of ALA in 1895/96. He composed these rules as part of a speech to teachers on the use of books.

 Read.

 Read.

03 Read some more.

 04 Read anything.

 05 Read about everything.

 06 Read enjoyable things.

 07 Read things you yourself enjoy.

 08 Read, and talk about it.

 09 Read very carefully, some things.

 10 Read on the run, most things.

 11 Don't think about reading, but

 12 Just read.

TOP 25 LARGEST LIBRARIES IN NORTH AMERICA

 LIBRARY OF CONGRESS (32.8 million volumes)

 HARVARD UNIVERSITY (16.2 million volumes)

 BOSTON PUBLIC LIBRARY (16.1 million volumes)

 YALE UNIVERSITY (12.5 million volumes)

 UNIVERSITY OF ILLINOIS AT URBANA-CHAMPAIGN (11.7 million volumes)

 UNIVERSITY OF TORONTO (11.2 million volumes)

 UNIVERSITY OF CALIFORNIA, BERKELEY (11.1 million volumes)

 COLUMBIA UNIVERSITY (10.3 million volumes)

 UNIVERSITY OF TEXAS AT AUSTIN (9.4 million volumes)

 PUBLIC LIBRARY OF CINCINNATI AND HAMILTON COUNTY (9.3 million volumes)

11 **UNIVERSITY OF MICHIGAN** (9.2 million volumes)

12 **NEW YORK PUBLIC LIBRARY** (9.1 million volumes)

13 INDIANA UNIVERSITY (8.7 million volumes)

14 UNIVERSITY OF CHICAGO (8.6 million volumes)

15 STANFORD UNIVERSITY (8.5 million volumes)

16 UNIVERSITY OF CALIFORNIA, LOS ANGELES (8.4 million volumes)

17 TORONTO PUBLIC LIBRARY (8.2 million volumes)

18 CANADA INSTITUTE FOR SCIENTIFIC AND TECHNICAL INFORMATION (8.2 million volumes)

19 CORNELL UNIVERSITY (8.1 million volumes)

20 UNIVERSITY OF WISCONSIN, MADISON (8.1 million volumes)

21 COUNTY OF LOS ANGELES PUBLIC LIBRARY (7.5 million volumes)

22 UNIVERSITY OF WASHINGTON (7.4 million volumes)

23 DETROIT PUBLIC LIBRARY (7.4 million volumes)

24 PRINCETON UNIVERSITY (6.9 million volumes)

25 UNIVERSITY OF ALBERTA (6.9 million volumes)

10 UNUSUAL RARE-BOOK GENRES

01 ARTILLERY ELECTION SERMONS were annual public orations delivered to militia gatherings in the American colonies and early republic that focused on military and defense concerns. *Example:* Samuel Cooper, *A Sermon Preached to the Ancient and Honourable Artillery Company in Boston, New-England, June 3, 1751: Being the anniversary of their election of officers* (Boston: Printed by J. Draper for J. Edwards and D. Gookin, 1751).

02 CAPTIVITY NARRATIVES were colonial and postcolonial women's accounts of their capture by Indians and assimilation into their culture. *See* Kathryn Zabelle Derounian-Stodola, ed., *Women's Indian Captivity Narratives* (New York: Penguin, 1998).

03 CHAPBOOKS were small, cheap pamphlets with paper bindings that were sold door-to-door in England and America from the seventeenth to the nineteenth centuries by itinerant peddlers or "chapmen." They were illustrated with woodcuts and contained tales such as "Jack the Giant Killer," ballads, nursery rhymes, historical incidents, biographies, tracts, dream analyses, palmistry, and astrology. Most were published anonymously and few were dated. *See* Victor E. Neuberg, *Chapbooks: A Guide to Reference Material on English, Scottish, and American Chapbook Literature of the Eighteenth and Nineteenth Centuries* (London: Woburn Press, 1971).

04 CLOG ALMANACS were a primitive kind of almanac or calendar, formerly used in Norway, Denmark, and England, made by cutting notches or runes on the four edges of a clog—a square piece of wood, brass, or bone about eight inches long that could be hung up in a room or attached to a walking stick. Also known as runic calendars or primstavs. *See* Gangleri, "Rune Calendars," May 23, 2007, www.gang leri.nl/articles/59/rune-calendars/.

05 COSTERIANA were fragments of books allegedly printed with pre-Gutenberg wooden blocks by Laurens Janszoon Coster (1370?–1440?) of Haarlem in the Netherlands. Some 200 titles, including a copy of Aelius Donatus's *Ars Minor*, have been attributed to Coster or his assistants. However, studies conducted on the paper and type of these materials reveal that these items were all printed between 1463 and 1480. *See* Antonius van der Linde, *The Haarlem Legend of the Invention of Printing by Lourens Janszoon Coster, Critically Examined* (London: Blades, East, and Blades, 1871).

06 HARLEQUINADES were the first printed movable books for children, in which the reader lifts a series of flaps on each page to see a different illustration. Developed by London bookseller Robert Sayer in 1765, the books often featured harlequin characters from slapstick pantomime theatrical performances of the era. Also known as turn-ups or metamorphosis books. *See* Ellen G. K. Rubin, "Pop-Up and Movable Books in the Context of History," April 2005, www.popup lady.com/mov-history.htm.

07 HORNBOOKS were children's primers of the fifteenth through eighteenth centuries that consisted of a thin sheet of vellum or paper mounted on an oblong piece of wood and covered with transparent horn. The wooden frame had a handle by which it was hung from a child's girdle. The sheet bore the alphabet; the vowels in a line, followed by the vowels combined with consonants in tabular form; numerals; and prayers. *See* Andrew W. Tuer, *History of the Horn-book* (New York: Charles Scribner's Sons, 1896).

08 PUSTAKAS were Sumatran books consisting of long strips of tree bark and dealing with magic, medicine, or law. Written in a brilliantly colored ink, pustakas were folded concertina fashion and tied together with a string of woven rushes. *See* P. V. Voorhoeve, "Batak Bark Books," *Bulletin of the John Rylands Library* 33, no. 2 (March 1951): 283–98.

09 ROBINSONADES were works describing an individual's or a community's survival without the aid of civilization, as on a desert island, after Daniel Defoe's *Robinson Crusoe* (1719). *Example:* Louis Boussenard, *The Crusoes of Guiana, or The White Tiger* (London: S. Low, Marston, Searle, and Rivington, 1883).

10 SPIRIT COMMUNICATIONS were works channeled by Spiritualist or New Age mediums and allegedly authored by disembodied entities. *Example:* John Ballou Newbrough, *Oahspe, a New Bible in the Words of Jehovih and His Angel Embassadors* (New York and London: Oahspe Publishing Association, 1882).

10 BOOK CURSES

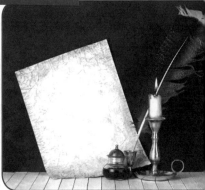

MEDIEVAL SCRIBES WHO made copies of manuscripts were expected to be completely accurate and use exactly the same number of pages and pagination as the original. The only space they had for their own comments was at the end of the manuscript, where they would customarily jot down the title of the work, the place where it was copied, or their own name. In this space, called the *colophon* (Greek for "finishing touch") or *explicit* (Latin for "the book is unrolled"), the scribe might also include a thanks to God for being done, complaints about how hard the work was, or an amusing verse. The tradition of the colophon extended into the era of movable type, when the space was used for information about the paper, design, typography, binding, and printer.

Occasionally the colophon was used to place a curse on anyone who altered or mutilated the text (in the case of theological works) or who stole the book (in the case of both sacred and secular works). The tradition of a book curse goes all the way back to the ancient Near East, perhaps the earliest being an inscription on the door of the temple library belonging to Sargon of Akkad (ca. 2250 BC), which read, "Whoever removes this inscribed stone, may Bel and Shamash tear out his foundation and exterminate his posterity." In medieval Europe, the curse sometimes called for an "anathema" on the perpetrator, which could be anything from excommunication from the church to infection with leprosy. Here are 10 diverting book curses, in more or less chronological order.

01 "Whoever alters a word of this codex . . . or erases one letter or rips off one leaf . . . may he have neither pardon nor forgiveness, neither 'let him behold the beauty of the Lord' (Psalms 27:4), nor 'let him see the good that is reserved for those who fear Him' (Jeremiah 29:32). He shall be like a woman in impurity and like a leprous man who has to be locked up so that his limbs may be crushed, the pride of his power broken, 'his flesh be consumed away that it cannot be seen and his bones corrode to unsightliness' (Job 33:21). Amen."
[From a note added to the colophon in the Codex Cairensis, written by Moses ben Asher in Tiberias in the year AD 895, thought to be the oldest extant Hebrew manuscript containing the complete text of the Old Testament books of the prophets.]

"Should anyone by craft or any device whatever abstract this book from this place, may his soul suffer in retribution for what he has done, and may his name be erased from the book of the living and not recorded among the Blessed."

[From an early eleventh-century missal that belonged to Robert of Jumièges, the first Norman Archbishop of Canterbury.]

"This is the book of St. James of Wigmore. If anyone takes it away or maliciously destroys this notice in taking it away from the above-mentioned place, may he be tied by the chain of greater excommunication. Amen. So be it. So be it. So be it."

[From a thirteenth-century manuscript of Petrus Riga's *Aurora,* a versified Latin paraphrase of the Bible, originally held by the Church of St. James, Wigmore, Herefordshire, and now in Trinity College Library, Cambridge, B.2.23 290.]

"May the sword of anathema slay / If anyone steals this book away."

[Found on the first folio of a fourteenth-century fragment of *Die vier Bücher der Könige.*]

"Whoever steals this book / Will hang on a gallows in Paris, / And, if he isn't hung, he'll drown, / And if he doesn't drown, he'll roast, / And if he doesn't roast, a worse end will befall him."

[Found on folio 116 of the fifteenth-century manuscript *La gene-alogie des roys du France,* from the library of Jean d'Orléans, comte d'Angoulême, in the Château des Valois in the commune of Cognac.]

"May he who wrote this book procure the joys of life supernal, / May he who steals this book endure the pangs of death infernal."

[From a book of Psalms dated 1444 in the explicit.]

"He that thys Boke renttes or steles / god send hym' sekenysse svart [sickness black] of helle."

[Added in a late fifteenth-century hand to the recto of the first folio in a late fourteenth-century manuscript of Chaucer's *Troilus and Criseyde,* Corpus Christi College Cambridge MS 61.]

"This book belongs to none but me / For there's my name inside to see. / To steal this book, if you should try, / It's by the throat that you'll hang high. / And ravens then will gather 'bout / To find your eyes and pull them out. / And when you're screaming 'oh, oh, oh!' / Remember, you deserved this woe."

[Inscribed in mixed Latin and German in an unnamed book, possibly dating from the nineteenth century, in the Germanisches Nationalmuseum in Nuremberg.]

09 "For him that stealeth a Book from this Library, let it change to a Serpent in his hand and rend him. Let him be struck with Palsy, and all his Members blasted. Let him languish in Pain, crying aloud for Mercy and let there be no surcease to his Agony till he sink to Dissolution. Let Book-worms gnaw his Entrails in token of the Worm that dieth not, and when at last he goeth to his final Punishment let the Flames of Hell consume him for ever and aye."

[Though widely quoted by many books and websites, this curse is actually a hoax. It first appeared in Edmund Lester Pearson's *The Old Librarian's Almanack,* written in 1909. However, Pearson was a literary humorist (and former librarian) who had written the "almanack" himself. He attributes the curse to a "Warning display'd in the Library of the Popish Monastery of San Pedro at Barcelona. This is the version English'd by Sir Matthew Manhan, who saw it writ in Latin in the Monastery, as he himself describes in his learn'd Book, *Travels in Spanish Countries, 1712.*" Although there is a San Pedro de Cardeña Monastery in Burgos, there apparently never was one at Barcelona, although the tenth-century Sant Pere (San Pedro in Catalan) de les Puelles monastery comes close. Sir Matthew Manhan is completely fictitious.]

10 "No part of this book may be reproduced, replicated, reiterated, duplicated, conduplicated, retyped, transcribed by hand (manuscript or cursive), read aloud and recorded on audio tape, platter, or disk, lipsynched, stored in a retrieval system, or transmitted in any form or by any means, including genetic, chemical, mechanical, optical, xerographic, holographic, electronic, stereophonic, ceramic, acrylic, or telepathic (except for that copying permitted by Sections 107 and 108 of U.S. Copyright Law and except by reviewers for the public press who promise to read the book painstakingly all the way through before writing their reviews) without prior written permission from the Publisher."

[This copyright statement in the front matter of Hillel Schwartz's *The Culture of the Copy* (New York: Zone Books, 1996) is clearly meant as a satire on restrictive copyright statements, which are indeed a modern form of the book curse.]

10 INTRIGUING PAPER DEFECTS

 BLEACH SCALE. Pearly, light brown, brittle spots in papers.

 CALENDER CUTS. Small wrinkles in the paper parallel to one of the sides.

 CONTRARIES. Any foreign substance in paper, such as sand, feathers, string.

 FEATHERED PAPERS. Papers whose deckled edges are quite large and thin.

 FISH EYES. Small, round, glazed spots in paper.

 HAIRCUTS. Hair-thin cuts in the surface of a sheet where it appears that hairs or long fibers have been pulled out of the surface.

 PHOZY. A featherweight paper with fibers too loosely pressed, yielding a light, weak sheet easy to tear.

 SNAILING. Streaks or snake-like marks on the surface of a sheet.

 VATMAN'S TEARS. Small, circular, thin spots, thicker around the circular edges, where a drop of water has dispersed the fibers in the hand-papermaking process.

 WINDER WELTS. Long, grain-direction ridges in the surface of the sheet.

STEPHEN LEARY'S TOP 10 WAYS TO EXIT A LIBRARY

THE NORMAL WAY (number 1) is to gather your things and proceed to the parking lot. But Stephen Leary, an information manager at a research institute in the Washington, D.C., area, has come up with some alternative scenarios.

 With books under your arm, properly checked out, your head held high, a confident gait.

 On a gurney, to an awaiting ambulance.

 Crawling on your belly underneath the barbed wire, pushing your books ahead of you in the dirt as you go.

 Nervously thanking and waving to the librarians at the circulation and reference desks as you beat a hasty retreat.

 Unnoticed through an obscured window way in the back, and into an awaiting getaway car filled with strange people.

 Handcuffed, gagged, drugged, and escorted by representatives of the CIA, Opus Dei, and ALA.

 Waving a brand new flag of an alien culture diametrically opposed to your own.

 Wearing an unbreakable mask designed and personally fitted for you by your favorite author.

 Shouting obscenities as you bump into the automatic doors that refuse to open for you.

 With your thralls holding you aloft in a modernist sedan chair, created entirely of pages torn from unpublished books authored by yourself.

BOOKLIST EDITORS' BEST
AMERICAN FICTION, 1980–2005

TITLES THAT RECEIVED two votes or more from *Booklist* editors, columnists, and reviewers, in order:

 MICHAEL CHABON, *The Amazing Adventures of Kavalier and Clay* (New York: Random House, 2000).

 WILLIAM KENNEDY, *Ironweed* (New York: Viking, 1983).

 LOUISE ERDRICH, *Love Medicine* (New York: Holt, Rinehart, and Winston, 1984).

 JOHN KENNEDY TOOLE, *A Confederacy of Dunces* (Baton Rouge: Louisiana State University, 1980).

 MARK HELPRIN, *Winter's Tale* (San Diego: Harcourt, Brace, Jovanovich, 1983).

 BARBARA KINGSOLVER, *Animal Dreams* (New York: HarperCollins, 1990).

 DON DELILLO, *Underworld* (New York: Scribner, 1997).

 DAVID FOSTER WALLACE, *Infinite Jest* (Boston: Little, Brown, 1996).

 TONI MORRISON, *Beloved* (New York: Alfred A. Knopf, 1987).

 PHILIP ROTH, *American Pastoral* (Boston: Houghton Mifflin, 1997).

 RICHARD POWERS, *The Gold Bug Variations* (New York: William Morrow, 1991).

TITLES THAT RECEIVED one vote:

 DAVID JAMES DUNCAN, *The Brothers K* (New York: Doubleday, 1992).

 SANDRA CISNEROS, *Caramelo, or Puro cuento* (New York: Alfred A. Knopf, 2002).

 SAUL BELLOW, *The Dean's December* (New York: Harper and Row, 1982).

 MARILYNNE ROBINSON, *Gilead* (New York: Farrar, Straus, and Giroux, 2004).

 MARILYNNE ROBINSON, *Housekeeping* (New York: Farrar, Straus, and Giroux, 1980).

 WENDELL BARRY, *Jayber Crow* (Washington, D.C.: Counterpoint, 2000).

 COLSON WHITEHEAD, *John Henry Days* (New York: Doubleday, 2001).

 GORE VIDAL, *Lincoln* (New York: Random House, 1984).

 ART SPIEGELMAN, *Maus: A Survivor's Tale* (New York: Pantheon, 1986).

 JOHN GARDNER, *Mickelsson's Ghosts* (New York: Alfred A. Knopf, 1982).

 DIANA GABALDON, *Outlander* (New York: Delacorte, 1991).

 JOHN UPDIKE, *Rabbit Is Rich* (New York: Alfred A. Knopf, 1981), and *Rabbit at Rest* (New York: Alfred A. Knopf, 1990).

 JOHN IRVING, *A Prayer for Owen Meany* (New York: William Morrow, 1989).

25 PHILIP ROTH, *The Plot against America* (Boston: Houghton Mifflin, 2004).

26 RICHARD FORD, *The Sportswriter* (New York: Vintage, 1986).

27 JANE SMILEY, *A Thousand Acres* (New York: Alfred A. Knopf, 1991).

TOP 10 CHALLENGED BOOKS, 1990–2000

A CHALLENGE IS an attempt to remove or restrict materials in a library, based upon the objections of a person or group. Challenges do not simply involve someone expressing a point of view; rather, they are an attempt to restrict the access of others. Due to the commitment of librarians, teachers, parents, students, and other concerned citizens, most challenges are unsuccessful and most materials are retained.

01 ALVIN SCHWARTZ, Scary Stories series: *Scary Stories to Tell in the Dark* (New York: Lippincott, 1981), *More Scary Stories to Tell in the Dark* (New York: Lippincott, 1984), and *Scary Stories 3: More Tales to Chill Your Bones* (New York: HarperCollins, 1991). Reasons: occultism/Satanism, religious viewpoint, violence.

 02 MICHAEL WILLHOITE, *Daddy's Roommate* (Boston: Alyson Wonderland, 1990). Reason: Homosexuality.

03 MAYA ANGELOU, *I Know Why the Caged Bird Sings* (New York: Random House, 1969). Reasons: offensive language, sexually explicit, unsuited to age group, violence.

04 ROBERT CORMIER, *The Chocolate War* (New York: Pantheon, 1974). Reasons: offensive language, religious viewpoint, sexually explicit, unsuited to age group, violence.

 05 MARK TWAIN, *The Adventures of Huckleberry Finn* (New York: Charles L. Webster, 1884). Reasons: racism, offensive language.

 06 JOHN STEINBECK, *Of Mice and Men* (New York: Covici Friede, 1937). Reason: offensive language.

07 J. K. ROWLING, Harry Potter series: *Harry Potter and the Philosopher's Stone* (London: Bloomsbury, 1997), *Harry Potter and the Chamber of Secrets* (London: Bloomsbury, 1998), *Harry Potter and the Prisoner of Azkaban* (London: Bloomsbury, 1999), *Harry Potter and the Goblet of Fire* (London: Bloomsbury, 2000). Reasons: occultism/Satanism, religious viewpoint, violence.

08 JUDY BLUME, *Forever . . .* (Scarsdale, N.Y.: Bradbury Press, 1975). Reasons: sexual content, offensive language.

09 KATHERINE PATERSON, *Bridge to Terabithia* (New York: Crowell, 1977). Reasons: occultism/Satanism, offensive language, violence.

10 PHYLLIS REYNOLDS NAYLOR, Alice series: *The Agony of Alice* (New York: Atheneum, 1985), *Alice in Rapture, Sort of* (New York: Atheneum, 1989), *Reluctantly Alice* (New York: Atheneum, 1991), and others. Reasons: homosexuality, offensive language, sexually explicit, unsuited to age group.

OTHER CHALLENGED BOOKS, 2001–2009

 JUSTIN RICHARDSON AND PETER PARNELL, *And Tango Makes Three* (New York: Simon and Schuster, 2005). Reasons: anti-ethnic, anti-family, homosexuality, religious viewpoint, unsuited to age group.

 ROBIE H. HARRIS, *It's Perfectly Normal: A Book about Changing Bodies, Growing Up, Sex, and Sexual Health* (Cambridge, Mass.: Candlewick, 1994). Reasons: homosexuality, nudity, sex education, religious viewpoint, abortion, unsuited to age group.

 PHILIP PULLMAN, His Dark Materials trilogy: *The Golden Compass* (New York: Alfred A. Knopf, 1996), *The Subtle Knife* (New York: Alfred A. Knopf, 1997), and *The Amber Spyglass* (New York: Alfred A. Knopf, 2000). Reasons: political viewpoint, religious viewpoint, violence.

 LAUREN MYRACLE, *ttyl* (New York: Amulet, 2004), and its sequels, *ttfn* (New York: Amulet, 2006), and *l8r, g8r* (New York: Amulet, 2007). Reasons: offensive language, sexually explicit, unsuited to age group.

 CECILY VON ZIEGESAR, Gossip Girls series: *Gossip Girl* (Boston: Little, Brown, 2002), *You Know You Love Me* (Boston: Little, Brown, 2002), *All I Want Is Everything* (New York: Little, Brown, 2003), and others. Reasons: homosexuality, sexually explicit, offensive language, unsuited to age group.

 J. D. SALINGER, *The Catcher in the Rye* (Boston: Little, Brown, 1951). Reasons: sexual content, offensive language, unsuited to age group.

 WALTER DEAN MYERS, *Fallen Angels* (New York: Scholastic, 1988). Reasons: offensive language, racism, violence.

 RUDOLFO A. ANAYA, *Bless Me, Ultima* (New York: Warner, 1972). Reasons: occultism/Satanism, offensive language, religious viewpoint, sexually explicit, violence.

STEPHEN CHBOSKY, *The Perks of Being a Wallflower* (New York: Pocket Books, 1999). Reasons: drugs, homosexuality, nudity, offensive language, sexually explicit, suicide, unsuited to age group.

 CAROLYN MACKLER, *The Earth, My Butt, and Other Big Round Things* (Cambridge, Mass.: Candlewick, 2003). Reasons: anti-family, offensive language, sexually explicit, unsuited to age group.

 STEPHENIE MEYER. *Twilight* series: *Twilight* (New York, Little, Brown, 2005); *New Moon* (New York: Little, Brown, 2006); *Eclipse* (New York: Little, Brown, 2007); and *Breaking Dawn* (New York: Little, Brown, 2008). Reasons: sexually explicit, religious viewpoint, unsuited to age group.

 JODI PICOULT. *My Sister's Keeper* (New York: Atria, 2004). Reasons: sexism, homosexuality, sexually explicit, offensive language, religious viewpoint, unsuited to age group, drugs, suicide, violence.

TOP 12 SILLY REASONS TO BAN A BOOK

 01 IT ACCURATELY DESCRIBES THE HISTORY OF LIFE ON EARTH. Juliet Clutton-Brock's *Horse* was challenged at the Smith Elementary School in Helena, Montana, in 2004 because a concerned parent said there were "too many questions with evolutionary theory to present it as a fact." She specifically objected to this passage: "It took about 55 million years for the present family of horses, asses, and zebras to evolve from their earliest horse-like ancestor."

02 IT CAUSES THE SLIGHTEST SUSPICION OF CONTROVERSY. Dee Brown's *Bury My Heart at Wounded Knee* was removed at Wild Rose, Wisconsin, in 1974 by a district administrator because the book was "slanted" and "if there's a possibility that something might be controversial, then why not eliminate it."

03 IT COULD LEAD TO PORNOGRAPHY. Maurice Sendak's *In the Night Kitchen* was challenged at the Elk River (Minn.) schools in 1992 because reading the book "could lay the foundation for future use of pornography."

04 IT ENCOURAGES CHILDREN TO BREAK DISHES. Shel Silverstein's *A Light in the Attic* was challenged in 1985 at the Cunningham Elementary School in Beloit, Wisconsin, because the book "encourages children to break dishes so they won't have to dry them."

 05 IT ENCOURAGES SUICIDE-INDUCED REINCARNATION. Laurence Yep's *Dragonwings* was challenged in the Apollo-Ridge schools in Kittanning, Pennsylvania, in 1992 because it might encourage children to "commit suicide because they think they can be reincarnated as something or someone else."

 06 IT HAS SMOKING ANIMALS. William Steig's *The Amazing Bone* was challenged at the West Armwell schools in Lambertville, New Jersey, in 1986 because of "the use of tobacco by the animals."

07 IT IS MUCH TOO FLATULENT. Glenn Murray's *Walter the Farting Dog* was challenged at the West Salem (Wis.) Elementary School in 2004 after a former school board member pointed out that the words *fart* and *farting* occur in the text 24 times. In a letter to the local newspaper, the board president explained that the school's mission to "help guide and nurture our youth into adulthood with some semblance of dignity and manners" is not served by the "graphical depiction of flatulence being blown into someone's face."

08 IT MIGHT CAUSE BUDDHISM TO ERUPT. D. T. Suzuki's *Zen Buddhism: Selected Writings* was challenged in the Plymouth-Canton (Mich.) Community school district in 1987 because "this book details the teachings of the religion of Buddhism in such a way that the reader could very likely embrace its teachings and choose this as his religion."

09 IT PREVENTS GOD FROM VISITING. A teacher's prayer group cautioned the Russell County, Kentucky, school board in 2002 that more than 50 books about ghosts, cults, and witchcraft "may need to be removed" from the high school library because God "cannot come into a place that is corrupted."

10 IT SHOWS CUBAN CHILDREN AS HAPPY. Alta Schreier's *Vamos a Cuba / A Voyage to Cuba* was challenged in the Miami–Dade County Public Schools in 2006 because it portrays a deceptively idealistic view of life in Cuba and depicts laughing Cuban children dressed in the uniform of the nation's Communist Party. The school board removed the book and the U.S. Supreme Court upheld the decision in 2009 because the book was "inaccurate." I don't know about the Justices, but I've been to Havana and seen smiling, uniformed schoolkids there. If inaccuracy is cause for removal, then many books in our nonfiction collections could be at risk.

11 IT SHOWS THAT TARZAN WAS NOT MARRIED TO JANE. Edgar Rice Burroughs's *Tarzan* was removed from the Los Angeles Public Library in 1929 because Tarzan was allegedly living in sin with Jane.

12 IT UNLEASHES LUST. The *Guinness Book of World Records 2001* was challenged in 2002 in the Waukesha, Wisconsin, schools because boys clued each other to photos of models in a bikini, diamond-studded underwear, and a short tube dress. "It could start with one picture or one magazine," a complainant said, citing serial killer Ted Bundy's claim that pornography drove him to murder.

10 MOST POPULAR CELEBRITY READ® POSTERS

 Shaquille O'Neal

 Denzel Washington

 Whoopi Goldberg

 Orlando Bloom

 Sean Connery

 Mel Gibson

 Twilight

 Kristi Yamaguchi

 Harrison Ford

 Tony Hawk

WHAT TO DO WHEN THE MEDIA CALLS

THESE TIPS AND talking points are suggestions from the ALA Public Information Office on how best to answer questions from radio, TV, print, and online journalists when they call to ask about news or events at your library. Some of these suggestions will also apply if you are appearing on a podcast or televised panel discussion.

GENERAL TIPS

 01 ASK QUESTIONS.** Determine the name of the publication or media outlet. Find out the story's theme, the reporter's angle, and the deadline. If you do not feel qualified to address the question or are uncomfortable with the approach, say so. Help the reporter find another source.

 02 BE CLEAR ABOUT WHOSE POSITION YOU ARE REPRESENTING—your own, your library's, or the American Library Association's.

03 BE PREPARED TO ANSWER THE STANDARD QUESTIONS of who, what, when, where, why, and how. Have supporting facts and examples on hand.

 04 PAUSE BEFORE ANSWERING to think about what you want to say and the best way to say it. Keep your comments positive and to the point. If you must say something negative, only say it once; never repeat.

05 KEEP YOUR ANSWERS SIMPLE AND BRIEF. Too much information can overwhelm the reporter or the audience—and it may keep you from being quoted.

 06 DON'T BE AFRAID TO ADMIT YOU DON'T KNOW. Reporters do not want incorrect information. Tell them you'll get the information and call back.

 07 NEVER SAY "NO COMMENT." Acceptable alternatives are "I'm sorry, I can't answer that" or "I'll let you know as soon as I know."

KNOW YOUR AUDIENCE (teens, seniors, business owners) and what their concerns are. Ask your interviewer if you aren't sure.

 KNOW YOUR KEY MESSAGE. What is the most important point you want the reporter to convey to the audience? Deliver it at the first opportunity and try to repeat it at least twice. Check the ALA website for a policy statement or fact sheet on a variety of topics.

 TALK, DON'T SPEAK. Use simple language. Avoid acronyms, jargon, and technical language.

 LIMIT YOURSELF TO THREE TALKING POINTS. In an interview, less is more. Keep your answers short, to the point, about 25 words or fewer (12 seconds). Let the interviewer ask the questions.

 USE STATISTICS SPARINGLY. People don't remember them.

 TELL STORIES AND USE REAL EXAMPLES to illustrate key points. Audiences remember good stories.

 LET YOUR ENTHUSIASM SHOW. Deliver your message in a way that makes people feel—not just think—that libraries are important.

STAY IN CONTROL

 ANTICIPATE THE QUESTIONS you will most likely be asked and have answers ready.

 ASK THE INTERVIEWER IN ADVANCE what questions you will be asked. Although many will not provide specifics, they will at least give you a general outline.

 SPEAK DELIBERATELY. Pause after you answer. It lends you authority and allows the interviewer time to react.

 NEVER ANSWER A QUESTION YOU DON'T FULLY UNDERSTAND. Say, "I'm not sure I understand the question. Are you asking . . . ?"

BEWARE OF MANIPULATION. Some reporters may ask leading questions, such as "So, you are saying that . . ." followed by an idea for your agreement. Make your own statement and use your own words.

REMEMBER THERE IS NO SUCH THING AS "OFF THE RECORD." Don't let a reporter trick you into saying more than you want to say.

 FOCUS THE INTERVIEWER by going back to your primary message: "The real issue is . . ."

 BUY YOURSELF TIME TO THINK by saying, "That's an excellent question" or "Let me think about that and come back to it."

 FLAG KEY THOUGHTS with words and phrases like "The most important point I want to make is . . ." or "This issue is critical because . . ."

 BRIDGE TO THE POSITIVE. When asked a negative question, answer briefly without repeating any charged or negative words. Then bridge to a positive message. For example: *Q.* "Isn't it true that librarians allow children to watch pornography on the Internet?" *A.* "Absolutely not. Our role is to help children learn to use the Internet wisely and to help guide them to all the great sites that are out there."

 LISTEN TO YOUR INTERVIEWER. Watch for the wandering eye, the bored look. Make adjustments. Change your pacing. Pause. Raise and lower your voice.

ESPECIALLY FOR RADIO AND TV

 USE LOTS OF EXPRESSION—highs and lows, enthusiasm. It's all in the voice. Use simple, colorful language that paints a picture for the listener. Tell stories, but keep them brief and to the point.

 BE BRIEF. Brevity is even more important with broadcast media. You may have less than 20 seconds to answer one question.

 CREATE VISUAL INTEREST. How you look on TV is as important as what you say. Keep an open face with eyebrows raised, maintain good posture, use hand gestures, and vary your vocal expression. All this helps establish you as a credible and enthusiastic spokesperson. Props—a book, poster, or large photo—can add interest.

 LOOK AT THE INTERVIEWER, not the camera or the audience, unless you are doing an interview by remote or the interviewer is behind the camera.

PRACTICE ACTIVE LISTENING. In a panel discussion, look at whoever is speaking. The camera may still be on you.

 PICTURE WHO YOUR AUDIENCE IS and speak directly to them—from your heart as well as your mind. Use stories and examples listeners can relate to.

 WEAR MORE MAKEUP THAN USUAL. Heavier lipstick and blush counteracts the harshness of the lights and still looks natural. Powder helps minimize shine. Some stations provide professional makeup assistance for both men and women.

 AVOID HARSH COLORS like black, navy, white, or bright red. Rich colors—bright blue, rust, wine, or purple—work well for most women, as does charcoal gray or brown for men. Dress as you would for a business meeting. A blouse and suit with an open collar is flattering for most women.

KEEP JEWELRY SIMPLE. Medium-sized earrings or a pin helps focus attention on the face. Avoid dangling earrings or necklaces that move or glitter when you talk; they distract from what you are saying.

USE GLASSES WITH NONREFLECTIVE LENSES, if possible.

HOW TO SAY "WHERE IS THE LIBRARY?" IN 50 LANGUAGES

ALBANIAN: "Ku është biblioteka?"
AMHARIC: "Betemesehaft yet new?"
ARABIC (KUWAITI): "Wään il maktaba?"
ARABIC (MOROCCAN): "Fin kein shī khīzana?"
AZERBAIJANI: "Kitabxana haradadir?"
BULGARIAN: "Kade e bibliotékta?"
CHINESE (CANTONESE): "To sùe gwóon hái bìn do ā?"
CHINESE (MANDARIN): "Túshūguǎn zài nǎr?"
CROATIAN: "Gdje je knjižnica?"
CZECH: "Kde je knihovna?"
DANISH: "Hvor er biblioteket?"
DUTCH: "Waar is de bibliotheek?"
ESTONIAN: "Kus on raamatukogu?"
FARSI (PERSIAN): "Ketābkhune kojāst?"
FINNISH: "Missä on kirjasto?"
FRENCH: "Où est la bibliothèque?"
GEORGIAN: "Sad aris biblioteka?"
GERMAN: "Wo ist der Bibliothek?"
GREEK: "Pou eínai ē bibliothékē?"
HAUSA: "I na laburari?"
HAWAIIAN: "Aia i hea ka hale puke?"
HEBREW: "Āfo ha sifriah?"
HINDI: "Pustakālay kidhar hai?"
HUNGARIAN: "Hol van a könyvtár?"
ICELANDIC: "Hvar er bókasafn?"
IRISH: "Cá bhfuil an leabharlann?"
ITALIAN: "Dov'è la biblioteca?"

JAPANESE: "Toshokan wa doko desu ka?"
KAZAKH: "Kitabkhana qayda?"
KOREAN: "Tosŏgwan ŏdie issŭmnikka?"
LATVIAN: "Kur atrodas bibliotēka?"
LITHUANIAN: "Kur yra biblioteka?"
MALAY: "Di mana perpustakaan?"
MALAYALAM: "Pustakalay eviteyaku nu?"
MONGOLIAN: "Nomyn sang khan bain ve?"
NEPALI: "Pustakālaya kasari jāne?"
PASHTO: "Cherta dai kitabkhāna?"
POLISH: "Gdzie jest w bibliotece?"
PORTUGUESE: "Onde está a biblioteca?"
ROMANIAN: "Unde este biblioteca?"
RUSSIAN: "Gde nakhoditsia biblioteka?"
SERBIAN: "Gde je biblioteka?"
SPANISH: "¿Dónde está la biblioteca?"
SWAHILI: "Maktaba iko wapi?"
SWEDISH: "Var är i biblioteket?"
TAGALOG: "Násaan ang silid aklatan?"
TAJIK: "Kujost kitobkhona?"
THAI: "Hong sa moot yùu tee nāi?"
TURKISH: "Burada kütüphane?"
UKRAINIAN: "De naxoditsia biblioteka?"
URDU: "Kutubkhānā kahan hain?"
VIETNAMESE: "Thư viện ở đâu?"

TOP 10 LIBRARY MUSIC VIDEOS

01 *AFRICA* (4:33). The video for this 1982 song by Los Angeles rock band Toto features singer David Paich in a law library, looking for truth as an African American librarian glares suspiciously at him. He pulls a book titled *Africa* off the shelf, unleashing some primal force. An African throws a spear, knocking over some books onto a lantern that sets the place on fire, perhaps in retribution for Paich's tearing out a bit of a page from the book. The band plays on a pile of gigantic books. (www.youtube.com/watch?v=lPT_3PEjnsE)

02 *EVERYTIME WE TOUCH* (3:21). This 2005 hit by German eurodance group Cascada features a stereotypical male librarian entranced by a lovely blonde (Cascada's Natalie Horler) who first gets him angry by strutting on the reading room table, pulling out card catalog drawers, and disorganizing library papers but then transforms him, nearby patrons, and the library janitor into dancin' fools. (www.youtube.com/watch?v=4G6QDNC4jPs)

03 *GUMDROPS IN THE LIBRARY* (2:07). This catchy bubblegum video stars a library, a librarian (played by Esse L. Maple), a fluffy library cat, a bunch of dancing kids, and a bunch of dancing Smittens. "Gumdrops" is from The Smittens' third album, *The Coolest Thing about Love*. Scenes were shot in the Lawrence Barnes Elementary School library in Burlington, Vermont. (www.youtube.com/watch?v=eyoR7Pch6Uo)

04 *HEAD OVER HEELS: LITERAL VIDEO VERSION* (3:06). The video for the 1985 hit song "Head Over Heels" by Tears for Fears centered around Roland Orzabal's attempts to get the attention of a librarian, played by Canadian model Joan Densmore. It was filmed in the Emmanuel College Library at the University of Toronto. In 2008, DustFilms mashed up the video using lyrics that more accurately match the words and thoughts of the characters with their on-screen antics. (www.funnyordie.com/videos/6342db2270/head-over-heels-literal-video-version-from-dustfilms)

05 *I WANT TO BE A LIBRARIAN* (6:02). It's the end of the 2008 term at the University of Alberta's School of Library and Information Studies and several first-year students are hard at work on a paper. Of course, they break out in song (a rewrite of "I Want to Be a Producer" from the 1968 Mel Brooks movie *The Producers*). Yes, the date/time, sound scale, and text on the screen are distracting, but it was shot by and edited by people who hadn't used a video camera before. (www.youtube.com/watch?v=o4TKDlgUliQ)

06 *LIBRARIAN* (4:10). This 2007 video by the New Zealand band Haunted Love was filmed in the lower basement stacks at Dunedin Public Library and released to coincide with a national library campaign. The band's Rainy McMaster and Geva Downey play the stereotypical librarians (using typewriters and rubber stamps), who nonetheless deal out revenge on a misbehaving patron who "has no understanding of library protocols." (www.youtube.com/watch?v=Ne_WXP7lUWM)

07 *LIBRARY 101* (7:38). Produced and performed by Michael Porter (WebJunction) and David Lee King (Topeka and Shawnee County Public Library), the video debuted at the Internet Librarian Conference in October 2009. Librarians "from around the world" sent in their photos, many holding signs with 1s and 0s, to be included in the video. (www.libraryman.com/library101/)

08 *MAGNUM A.L.* (1:27). This video showcased the crack editorial team at *American Libraries* during their centennial year of 2007. Using the *Magnum P.I.* theme song, this "gritty, action-packed thrill ride" directed and filmed by Daniel Kraus was one of the first videos in the AL Focus series. (http://alfocus.ala.org/videos/magnum-al/)

09 *SENECA LIBRARY HOLIDAY SONG* (4:50). Mikey Mike (AV technician Michael London) and the Library Bunch sing the praises of the library at the Markham campus of Toronto's Seneca College in this jazzy holiday number. "Shhh, you gotta keep your voices down, people need a place to read." (www.youtube.com/watch?v=cMVMgDWnoaA)

10 *THRILLER* (5:26). The National Library of Australia staff knows how to put on a holiday party. Each year they hold festivities in the public foyer where the talents of librarians, archivists, shelvers, communication experts, digital specialists, and IT techies are displayed. In 2008, they performed an amusing library version of Michael Jackson's "Thriller" (www.youtube.com/watch?v=DPhM7JbsgxU), wherein the librarian character undergoes an inspiring transformation. In 2009, the "Can Can't" dancers put on a boisterous recital using office chairs and book carts (www.youtube.com/watch?v=UzjYccj65Tk). The 2007 party featured the "Surfing NLA" team (www.youtube.com/watch?v=lvKntJKctoU) using bookcarts as surfboards.

NOTES

PAGE 1: George M. Eberhart, ed., *The Whole Library Handbook 4* (Chicago: American Library Association, 2006), 2.

PAGE 2: Octave Uzanne and Albert Robida, *Contes pour les bibliophiles* (Paris: Quantin, 1895), 125–45; "Visions de l'an 2000," part of an online exhibition at the Bibliothèque Nationale de France, http://expositions.bnf.fr/utopie/ grand/3_95b1.htm; "Thinking Men and Women Predict Problems of World a Century Hence," *Bridgeport (Conn.) Telegram,* February 12, 1923; Jorge Luis Borges, "La biblioteca de Babel," in *El Jardín de senderos que se bifurcan* (Buenos Aires: Editorial Sur, 1942); Vannevar Bush, "As We May Think," *Atlantic Monthly* (July 1945): 101–8; J. C. R. Licklider, *Libraries of the Future* (Cambridge, Mass.: MIT Press, 1965), 6; Thomas J. Hennen Jr., "Public Librarians Take Cool View of Future," *American Libraries* 19 (May 1988): 390; Frederick Wilfrid Lancaster, ed., *Libraries and the Future: Essays on the Library in the Twenty-first Century* (New York: Haworth, 1993), 80.

PAGE 4: Terry Pratchett, *Guards! Guards!* (New York: HarperTorch, 1989), 223.

PAGE 5: People for a Library-Themed Ben & Jerry's Flavor!, www.facebook.com/ group.php?gid=88574048291.

PAGE 7: Image courtesy of the Wainfleet Township Public Library, Wainfleet, Ontario.

PAGE 9: Bring Back Ms Dewey, www.facebook.com/home.php#/group.php?gid= 85888907592.

PAGE 11: Danielle Dreger-Babbitt, "Top 20 Things Librarians in Public Libraries Wish Their Patrons Knew or Did," Examiner.com, November 18–21, 2008, www .examiner.com/x-1361-Seattle-Books-Examiner. Reprinted with permission.

PAGE 13: Brian Herzog, "Top 10 Patron Pet Peeves," *Swiss Army Librarian,* June 2, 2009, www.swissarmylibrarian.net/2009/06/02/top-10-patron-pet-peeves. Reprinted with permission.

PAGE 16: Henry T. Coutts, *Library Jokes and Jottings* (London: Grafton, 1914), 84–86.

PAGE 18: Janice M. Hughes, *The ROM Field Guide to Birds of Ontario* (Toronto: Royal Ontario Museum, 2001), 265; Peter Slater, Pat Slater, and Raoul Slater, *The Slater Field Guide to Australian Birds* (Willoughby, N.S.W.: Lansdowne-Rigby, 1986), 192, 236, 260; Morten Strange, *A Photographic Guide to the Birds of Southeast Asia Including the Philippines and Borneo* (Hong Kong:

Periplus, 2000), 103; Orlando H. Garrido and Arturo Kirkconnell, *Field Guide to the Birds of Cuba* (Ithaca, N.Y.: Cornell University, 2000), 201.

PAGE 19: Original contribution by Larry Nix. Visit his website at www.library historybuff.org.

PAGE 21: All items are from my own collection. For more information on library postcards, see the *Library Postcards* blog (http://librarypostcards.blogspot .com) maintained by Mark Jackson, reference and online resources librarian at Bloomfield (N.J.) College Library. Judy Aulik, Downers Grove (Ill.) Public Library reference librarian, has a wonderful site called Library Postcards: Civic Pride in a Lost America (http://home.comcast.net/~jaulik/ index.html). Sjoerd Koopman, professional programs director for the International Federation of Library Associations and Institutions in The Hague, Netherlands, donated digital images of his vast collection of U.S. library postcards to the ALA Archives at the University of Illinois at Urbana-Champaign; they are accessible at http://images.library.uiuc.edu:8081/ cdm4/browse.php?CISOROOT=/koopman. Visit Larry Nix's Library History Buff website (www.libraryhistorybuff.org/postcards.htm) for more links to postcard resources as well as Larry's blog (http://libraryhistorybuff.blogspot .com).

PAGE 40: Original contribution by Norman D. Stevens, director emeritus of the University of Connecticut Library in Storrs.

PAGE 44: Some titles are from the *Bookseller*/Diagram Prize for Oddest Book Title of the Year, others are from Russell Ash and Brian Lake, *Bizarre Books* (New York: Harper Perennial, 2007), while still others are from my own collection.

PAGE 46: Adapted from Martha J. Spear, "The Top 10 Reasons to Be a Librarian," *American Libraries* 33 (October 2002): 54–55.

PAGE 47: Scott Douglas, "Dispatches from a Public Librarian: Dispatch 28," McSweeney's Internet Tendency, March 3, 2008, www.mcsweeneys.net/ links/librarian/3prosandcons.html. Reprinted with permission. Douglas is the author of *Quiet, Please: Dispatches from a Public Librarian* (Cambridge, MA: Da Capo, 2008).

PAGE 49: Jennifer Friedman. Reprinted with permission.

PAGE 51: Emma Bradford Perry, "Let Recruitment Begin with Me," *American Libraries* 35 (May 2004): 36–38.

PAGE 52: Roy Tennant, "The Top 10 Things That Library Administrators Should Know about Technology," *TechEssence.info,* September 12, 2009, http:// techessence .info/topten/. Reprinted with permission.

PAGE 55: Leigh Anne Vrabel, "10 Things I Will Do When I Am Library Director," *Library Alchemy,* October 28, 2009, http://libraryalchemy.wordpress.com. Reprinted with permission.

PAGE 58: Original contribution from Jenny Levine, updated from a post on *The Shifted Librarian,* August 23, 2007, http://theshiftedlibrarian.com.

PAGE 60: Original contribution by Sean Fitzpatrick.

PAGE 62: Elizabeth W. Stone, *American Library Development, 1600–1899* (New York: H. W. Wilson, 1977); ALA Professional Tips wiki, http://wikis.ala.org/ professionaltips/index.php/Firsts; Matthew Reidsma, "852: Rare—Harvard,

It's in the Cards," *Et Seq.,* October 27, 2008, http://etseq.law.harvard.edu; Larry Nix, "Free Public Libraries 160 Years," *Library History Buff Blog,* July 9, 2009, http://libraryhistorybuff.blogspot.com; Anthony M. Wilson and Robert Hermanson, "Educating and Training Library Practitioners," *Library Trends* 46 (Winter 1998): 467–504; Arthur E. Bostwick, *The American Public Library* (New York: D. Appleton, 1910), 12; Jesse Shera, *Foundations of the Public Library* (Chicago: University of Chicago, 1949), 132–33; Maurice Wheeler and Debbie Johnson-Houston, "A Brief History of Library Service to African Americans," *American Libraries* 35 (February 2004): 42–45; George M. Eberhart, "Things We Use in Libraries and When They Were Invented," *The Whole Library Handbook 4* (Chicago: American Library Association, 2006), 418–16; Jay Singh, Navjit Brar, and Carmen Fong, "The State of RFID Applications in Libraries," *Information Technology and Libraries* 25, no. 1 (March 2006): 24–32; "Anythink Brighton Becomes the First Carbon Positive Library in the U.S.," December 2009, www.anythink libraries.org.

PAGE 73: Stephen C. Hill, "Ghost Hunters Come to Belchertown Library," Northampton (Mass.) *Daily Hampshire Gazette,* November 27, 2007; Barbara Stagg, personal interview, 1997; George M. Eberhart, "Phantoms among the Folios: A Guide to Haunted Libraries," *American Libraries* 28 (October 1997): 68–71; Charles J. Adams III, *Philadelphia Ghost Stories* (Reading, Pa.: Exeter House, 1998), 58–64; Daniel W. Barefoot, *Haunted Halls of Ivy* (Winston-Salem, N.C.: J. F. Blair, 2004), 20; Angie Froese, "The True Story of Ida Day Holzapfel," *Hutchinson Collegian,* October 21, 2001; John B. Kachuba, *Ghosthunting Ohio* (Cincinnati: Emmis Books, 2004), 49–52; David Eggert, "Paying Tribute to Caring Librarian's Life—and Afterlife," *Seattle Post-Intelligencer,* May 25, 2002; Troy Taylor, "The Ghost of Angie Milner," History and Hauntings of Illinois, www.prairieghosts.com/ milner.html, 2000; Erin Plummer, "Ghosts May Haunt Meredith Library," *Laconia (N.H.) Citizen,* October 1, 2008; Alan Brown, *Haunted Places in the American South* (Jackson: University Press of Mississippi, 2002), 5–9; Chris Woodyard, *Haunted Ohio IV* (Beavercreek, Ohio: Kestrel, 1997), 173–74.

PAGE 80: For more librarian poets, see *Leaves of Bark: Of Bards and Bookworms,* http://deadpoets.typepad.com/leaves_of_bark/.

PAGE 82: Adapted from "12 Ways Libraries Are Good for the Country," *American Libraries* 26 (December 1995): 1113–19.

PAGE 84: Adapted from S. R. Ranganathan, *The Five Laws of Library Science* (1st ed., Madras [modern Chennai], India: Madras Library Association, 1931).

PAGE 85: Walt Crawford and Michael Gorman, *Future Libraries: Dreams, Madness, and Reality* (Chicago: American Library Association, 1995), 7–8.

PAGE 86: The rules were printed in the Report of the Sedalia (Mo.) Public Library for 1924 but were apparently composed earlier. They also appear in Frank Kingdon's *John Cotton Dana: A Life* (Newark, N.J.: Public Library and Museum, 1940), 123; and *Library Journal* 58 (1933): 821.

PAGE 88: *Annual Report of the Librarian of Congress* (Washington, D.C.: Library of Congress, 2008), www.loc.gov/about/reports/annualreports/fy2008.pdf; *ARL Statistics 2007–2008* (Washington, D.C.: Association of Research Libraries, 2008); *Public Library Data Service Statistical Report 2009* (Chicago: Public Library Association, 2009); Stanford Facts: Libraries and Computing, www .stanford.edu/about/facts/libraries.html.

NOTES

PAGE 92: William Albert Mason, *A History of the Art of Writing* (New York: Macmillan, 1920), 258–59; Leila R. Avrin, *Scribes, Script, and Books: The Book Arts from Antiquity to the Renaissance* (Chicago: American Library Association, 1991), 128; Henry Austin Wilson, ed., *The Missal of Robert of Jumièges* (London: Henry Bradshaw Society, 1896), 316; Marc Drogin, *Anathema! Medieval Scribes and the History of Book Curses* (Totowa, N.J.: Allanheld and Schram, 1983), 68, 70, 90–91, 106–7; Wilhelm Wattenbach, *Das Schriftwesen im Mittelalter* (Leipzig: S. Hirzel, 1896), 527–29, 534; Friedrich Jacobs and Friedrich August Ukert, *Beiträge zur ältern Litteratur oder Merkwürdigkeiten der Herzoglichen öffentlichen Bibliothek zu Gotha* (Leipzig: Dyk'sche Buchhandlung, 1836), Bd. 2, pp. 19, 49–50; Denis Jean Achille Luchaire, *Mélanges d'histoire du Moyen Age* (Paris: Félix Alcan, 1897), vol. 3, pp. 41–42, 62; F. Adams, "Book Inscription," *Notes and Queries,* ser. 9, 1 (January 29, 1898): 86; Montague Rhodes James, *The Western Manuscripts in the Library of Trinity College, Cambridge* (Cambridge: University Press, 1900–1904), vol. 1, p. 80; Leslie K. Arnovick, *Written Reliquaries: The Resonance of Orality in Medieval English Texts* (Amsterdam: J. Benjamins, 2006), 210; Edmund Lester Pearson, *The Old Librarian's Almanack by Φιλόβιβλος: A Very Rare Pamphlet First Published in New Haven Connecticut in 1773 and Now Reprinted for the First Time* (Woodstock, Vt.: Elm Tree Press, 1909), [10]; Michael Saucrs, "Funniest Copyright Statement Ever," *The Travelin' Librarian,* February 26, 2008, www.travelinlibrarian.info.

PAGE 95: ALA/ACRL Rare Books and Manuscripts Section, *Paper Terms: A Thesaurus for Use in Rare Book and Special Collections Cataloguing* (Chicago: American Library Association, 1990).

PAGE 96: Stephen Leary, "Top 10 Ways to Leave a Library," *The Leary Letter,* June 7, 2006, http://blog.stephenleary.com/2006/06/top-10-ways-to-leave-library.html. Reprinted with permission.

PAGE 97: Bill Ott, *The Back Page* (Chicago: American Library Association, 2009), 105–6.

PAGE 100: ALA Office for Intellectual Freedom, 100 Most Frequently Challenged Books: 1990–2000, www.ala.org/ala/issuesadvocacy/banned/frequentlychallenged/challengedbydecade/1990_2000.cfm.

PAGE 102: ALA Office for Intellectual Freedom.

PAGE 104: Robert P. Doyle, *Banned Books: 1994 Resource Guide* (Chicago: American Library Association, 1994); George M. Eberhart, *The Whole Library Handbook 3* (Chicago: American Library Association, 2000), 461; George M. Eberhart, *The Whole Library Handbook 4* (Chicago: American Library Association, 2006), 471.

PAGE 106: Based on quantity sold by ALA Graphics. READ is a trademark of the American Library Association. READ® "Superhero" background from READ DVD "Genres and Subjects" by ALA Graphics.

PAGE 107: The ALA Public Information Office.

You may also be interested in

The Whole Library Handbook 4: Readers will find fascinating bits of trivia, as well as humorous sections on "how many academic librarians does it take to change a lightbulb?" and "advice from naughty library assistants." Also included are thoughtful essays and reprints of important journal articles by noted experts.

The Librarian's Book of Quotes: Celebrate librarianship and the love of libraries with this charming collection of quotes. Tatyana Eckstrand has compiled nearly three hundred of the most insightful, thought-provoking, and inspiring aphorisms about the library profession.

The Back Page: Where else can you find an entertaining book filled with the miscellany of the publishing world? Readers can discover everything from the trivial to the important in Bill Ott's *The Back Page*, part readers' advisory and part commentary on the world of books and literature, good and not so good.

The Library: Illustrated with 130 rich color photos, readers can follow the fascinating progress of the institution we now know today as the library. A rich textual and visual resource, *The Library* will delight patrons and library staff alike.

Order today at www.alastore.ala.org or 866-746-7252!

ALA Store purchases fund advocacy, awareness, and accreditation programs for library professionals worldwide.